Take the Challenge;
Leave not a trace of your visit behind.

In order to preserve the unique features of the Monument and other backcountry destinations for the future, become a no-trace user and camper. Through practicing a minimum-impact ethic you can hone your outdoor skills and increase your awareness. Here's the Challenge:

Selecting a campsite:
• Camp in designated areas, where established.
• Choose an existing campsite at least 100 feet from lakeshores or streams.
• Choose wooded areas instead of meadows.
• Pitch your tent on well-drained soils to avoid trenching.
• Maintain privacy by camping away from others.

Washing up:
• When washing yourself, dishes, or brushing teeth, collect water and carry it 200 feet away from the water source before carrying out your task.
• Allow the "waste" water to percolate through absorbent soil. Even biodegradable soap is a stress on the environment.

Sanitation:
• Dig a hole several inches deep, 100 feet or more away from any water source. Place human waste and toilet paper in the hole and cover with soil. Waste will biodegrade most quickly if in the organic soil layer, three to eight inches below surface.

Drinking water:
• No longer can one confidently drink from mountain streams or lakes. The water may be contaminated with giardia or other harmful bacteria. For your safety, treat all water. On many trails the water supply is limited or unavailable. Come prepared!

Exposure:
• **Trails in the blast area are open and exposed. Carry sunscreen, water, and a hat.**

Litter:
• Pack out all of your litter and as much as possible of that left by others.

Camp Stoves/Campfires:
• Within the blown-down forest, campfires are prohibited; come prepared to cook on a camp stove.
• In areas where campfires are permitted and firewood is plentiful, use an existing ring for a small cooking fire.
• Collect only down and dead wood. Make sure your campfire is dead out and clean the fire ring of all trash. Burn only paper; pack out other materials.

Restricted Areas:
Trails located in Class I Research areas have special restrictions that apply. Restricted Areas are closed to off-trail travel and camping. Take the time to find out if the trail you've selected passes through these areas. Please adhere to the restrictions and preserve the fragile story these areas reveal to scientists and visitors.

Solitude:
• Preserve the solitude of the setting by camping out of sight of other parties and minimizing noise.
• Select "low-use" trails on weekends and visit "high-use" trails during weekdays, off-season or cloudy weather.

Preservation:
Remember to take only pictures and leave only footprints. As tempting as it might be to take home souvenirs of Mount St. Helens, don't become a Pumice Picker! (It is prohibited by law.) The pumice provides essential shade to the small seedlings that are aiding in the recovery of the area.

Special Challenges for Specific Users!

Pack and Saddle Users:
Preserve the beauty of the land and protect its natural features by following these guidelines:
• Stay on the trail and avoid wet and marshy areas.
• Use high picket lines, rope corrals; or hobble stock during overnight stays.
• Scatter manure at campsites and stops along the trail.
• Share the trail with others. Your friendliness will be remembered.
• Respect closed and restricted areas. Trails within the blast area are closed to pack and saddle use.

Motorized Trail Bike Users:
To ensure that your and other users' experiences are rewarding, please adhere to these tips and restrictions:
• Preserve the beauty of mountain areas by treading lightly upon the land.
• Keep your trail bike within quiet standards and your spark arrestor in place.
• Avoid using trails during the wet season.
• Remain on the trail! Resist the urge to pioneer new trails across meadows, near lake shores or stream banks.
• Use courtesy when you meet other users on the trail. Pull off and give the right of way to pack and saddle users or hikers.
• Be informed as to which trails are open to trail bikes.

Mountain Bike Users:
For the enjoyment and safety of your ride and to respect the land and other users, please remember these guidelines:

• Stay on the trail. Help protect the trail by not skidding tires or locking up brakes on the trails.
• Maintain a safe speed at all times. Slow down and enjoy the beauty. Always use extra caution on curves, steep slopes and narrow trails.
• Share the trail, yield to hikers and uphill traffic. Avoid surprises by saying "hello."
• Some trails within the Monument are closed to mountain bikes. Please check with Monument Headquarters concerning mountain bike use.

Safety!

Be prepared:
• Bring the ten essentials:
1. Map and knowledge of the trail you're hiking. Let someone know of your destination and your return time.
2. Flashlight
3. Extra food
4. Extra clothing
5. Sunglasses/sunscreen/hat for blast area
6. First aid kit
7. Pocket knife
8. Waterproof matches, candles, fire starter
9. Water or the means to purify water (some areas are hot and dry in the summer)
10. Tarp, tent or emergency shelter

Safety Information

All hikers are responsible for their own safety. The following information may be crucial for your safety and for those who are with you. Please become familiar with this information.

Potential Volcanic Hazards

Mount St. Helens is an active volcano. Travelers should be aware of the potential hazards of hiking on the flanks of the volcano. These hazards are in addition to those normal hazards associated with high mountain travel such as changing weather, loose rock, and limited water.

Potential volcanic hazards while hiking on or near the flanks of Mount St. Helens may include the following:
• Steam explosions can hurl large rocks onto the flanks of the mountain.
• Volcanic ash can be spread miles from the volcano by even small eruptions and explosions.
• Melting snow can send torrents of debris down streams that drain the crater.

Steam bursts and small ash eruption events are likely to recur in the future and may occur without any prior warning. In the event of an eruption, these are some actions you can take to protect yourself:
• Hide behind large rocks for protection from flying debris.
• Protect your eyes from ash and debris.
• Use moistened clothing across your mouth and nose to minimize ash ingestion.
• Leave drainages as quickly as possible to avoid torrents of melted snow and debris.

How to select a trail:

From the serenity of an old-growth forest to the cascading crest of a waterfall, from the power of the blast zone to the awe of the steaming dome of lava, Mount St. Helens National Volcanic Monument offers the trail experience just right for you. Before stepping into this diverse landscape, let's take a moment to discover how to select a trail suited to your interests and abilities. To assist you in this process a Trail Tree has been developed. It categorizes the trails according to the "experience" you desire. Sections are broken down into Volcanic Landscapes (within the blast zone) and Forested Areas (unaffected by the eruption). Beneath these headings are "High Country View," "Lakes, Rivers, Waterfalls," "Big (Old-Growth) Trees," and "Lava Flows." The trails are then listed as being over or under three miles in length. After each trail's name and number, pertinent facts concerning types of users, exact length one-way and difficulty rating are given. For more in-depth information about your trail selection, turn to the trail's description (listed in numerical order). These contain scenic, historic and geologic points of interest, geographical locations, and important considerations. A map of the trail, its connection to other trails, and its main access points are also included.

By using this process of selection, you may feel confident that you will have an experience that will become a lasting and enjoyable memory. Come and discover which trail at Mount St. Helens is right for you.

Map and Symbol Key

🅰	Picnic Area	- - - -	Main Trail
🅿	Developed Parking	- - - - -	Connecting Trail
🅰	Campground	- - - - - - - -	Planned Trail
🅰	Restrooms	- - - - -	Restricted Area Trail
📷	Viewpoint	━━━	Paved Road
♿	Barrier Free	━ ━ ━	Gravel Road
🥤	Drinking Water	────	River
🚶	Interpretive Trail	••••••••••	Restricted Area
🛈	Information Station		
🚶	Hiking		
👫	Family Hiking		
🐎	Horseback		
🚲	Mountain Bike		
🏍	Trail Bike		
⛷	X-Country Skiing		
🧗	Caving		

Note: Map scales are approximate.

Trail Difficulty Definitions:

Easiest: Level to gently rolling. Easy hiking, suitable for children or individuals seeking a leisurely walk.

More Difficult: Vigorous hiking with moderate hills and slopes.

Most Difficult: Steep grades, narrow tread widths, low levels of maintenance. May require stepping over logs or traversing steep cliffs or stream fords. Trails may be difficult to locate or follow. Suitable for experienced hikers in good physical condition. Expect a challenging experience.

Alphabetical Trail Index

Forested Paths

High Country Views

over 3 miles

Craggy Peak Trail #3
4.5 miles
Page 26

Summit Prairie Trail #2
9 miles
Page 24

Goat Mountain Trail #217
10 miles
Page 110

Tumwater Trail #218
9 miles
Page 112

Boundary Trail #1
Elk Pass to Yellow Jacket
8 miles
Page *20*

Boundary Trail #1
Yellow Jacket to Council Lake
13.8 miles
Page 22

Strawberry Mt. Trail #220
10.7 miles
Page 114

Wright Meadow Trail #80
7.8 miles
Page 64

under 3 miles

Pine Creek Shelter #216C
0.4 miles
Page 86

Butte Camp Trail #238A
2.7 miles
Page 136

Stabler Camp Trail #17
2.6 miles
Page 38

House Rock Trail #6
0.5 miles
Page 36

Vanson Peak Trail #217A
1.4 miles
Page 110

over 3 miles (cont.)

Spencer Butte Trail #30
3.2 miles
Page 50

Cussed Hollow #19
3.3 miles
Page 42

Snagtooth Trail #4
4.8 miles
Page 28

Water

over 3 miles

Lewis River Trail #31
Curly Creek to Quartz Creek Trail
14.4 miles
Page 56, 58

Table Mountain Trail #18
5 miles
Page 40

Green River Trail #213
7.5 miles
Page 78

Quartz Creek Trail #5
10.6 miles
Page 30

Toutle Trail #238
Kalama segment
5.6 miles
Page 132

Goat Creek Trail #205
6 miles
Page 68

Blue Lake Horse Trail #237
5.25 miles
Page 130

Big Trees

under 3 miles | **over 3 miles** | **under 3 miles**

June Lake Trail #216B
1.6 miles
Page 84

Toutle Trail #238
Blue Lake segment
0.5 miles
Page 134

Middle Falls Trail #31C
0.8 miles loop
Page 60

Big Creek Falls Trail #28
0.7 miles
Page 48

Curly Creek Falls Trail #31
0.2 miles
Page 54

French Creek Trail #5C
3.25 miles
Page 34

Lewis River Trail #31
Curly Creek to Quartz Creek Trail
14.4 miles
Page 56, 58

Green River Trail #213
7.5 miles
Page 78

Quartz Creek Trail #5
10.6 miles
Page 30

French Creek Trail #5C
3.25 miles
Page 34

Goat Creek Trail #205
6 miles
Page 68

Vanson Ridge Trail #213A
3.3 mile
Page 80

Sheep Canyon trail #240
2.3 miles
Page 140

Toutle Trail #238
Blue Lake segment
0.5 miles (8 miles total)
Page 134

Pine Creek Shelter Trail #216C
0.4 miles
Page 86

Big Creek Falls Trail #28
0.7 miles
Page 48

Speed Trail #31E
1 mile
Page 62

Quartz Creek Butte #5B
1.5 miles
Page 32

Bluff Trail #24
2.7 miles
Page 44

Volcanic Landscapes

📷 High Country Views

over 3 miles | over 3 miles (cont.) | under 3 miles

Ape Canyon Trail #234
5.5 miles
Page 128

Truman Trail #207
6.5 miles
Page 70

Independence Pass Trail #227
3.5 miles
Page 122

Smith Creek Trail #225
9 miles
Page 120

Boundary Trail #1
Bear Meadow to Norway Pass Trailhead
4 miles
Page 18

Boundary Trail #1
Norway Pass Trailhead to Truman Trail
13.2 miles
Page 14

Loowit Trail #216
27.3 miles
Pages 94-109

Toutle Trail #238
Red Rock Pass Segment
8 miles
Page 132

Coldwater Trail #230
4.5 miles
Page 124

Windy Ridge Sand Ladder
0.25 miles, 365 steps
Page 142

Abraham Trail #216D
2 miles
Page 88

Boundary Trail #1
Norway Pass Trailhead to Norway Pass
2.2 miles
Page 16

Harmony Trail #224
1 mile
Page 118

Sheep Canyon Trail #240
2.2 miles
Page 140

Castle Ridge Trail #216G
2 miles
Page 92

Water
Lava Flows 🌋

Climbing

Permit Required
above 4800 feet

under 3 miles   under 3 miles

Meta Lake Trail #210
0.25 miles
Page 74

Trail of Two Forests #233
0.25 mile Boardwalk
Page 126

Ptarmigan Trail #216A
2.2 miles to 4800 feet
Page 82

Harmony Trail #224
1 mile
Page 118

Ape Cave Trail #239
Page 128

Surface Trail 1.25 miles

Upper Passage 1.25 miles

Lower Passage 1.5 miles
Round Trip

Butte Camp Trail #238A
2.8 miles
Page 136

Ghost Lake Trail #1H
0.5 miles
Page 18

Sheep Canyon Trail #240
2.2 miles to 4800 feet
Page 140

Castle Lake Trail #221
4 miles
Page 116

Lava Canyon Trail #184
Page 66

Upper 0.5 miles

Middle Loop 0.5 miles

Lower 2.0 miles

Lava Canyon Trail #184
Page 66

Upper 0.5 miles

Middle Loop 0.5 miles

Lower 2.0 miles

Water
over 3 miles

Lakes Trail #211
5 miles
Page 76

Boundary Trail #1
and Connecting Trails

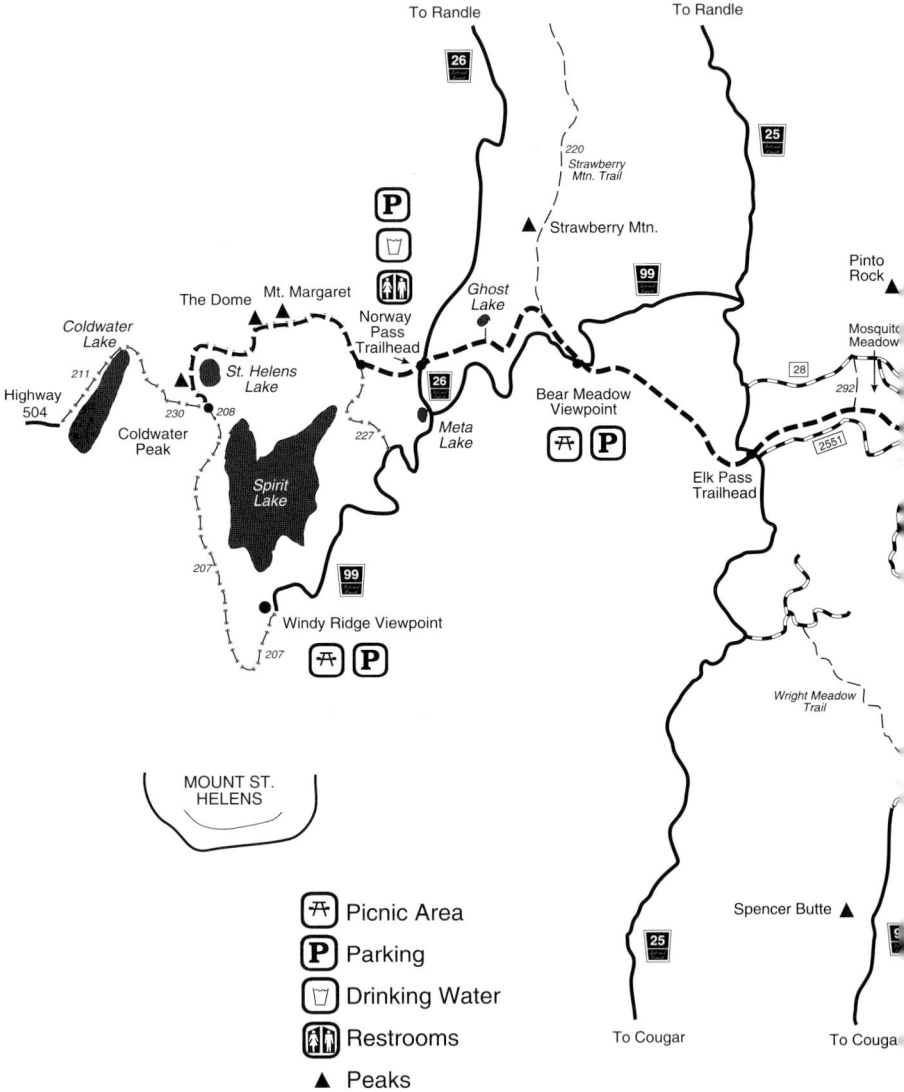

To Randle

To Randle

26

25

220
Strawberry
Mtn. Trail

P

▲ Strawberry Mtn.

Pinto
Rock ▲

99

Mosquito
Meadow

The Dome   Mt. Margaret

Coldwater
Lake

▲   ▲

Ghost
Lake

28

Norway
Pass
Trailhead

292

211

▲   St. Helens
Lake

Highway
504

26

Bear Meadow
Viewpoint

2551

230   208

Meta
Lake

Elk Pass
Trailhead

Coldwater
Peak

227

🏔 P

Spirit
Lake

207

99

207

Windy Ridge Viewpoint

🏔 P

Wright Meadow
Trail

MOUNT ST.
HELENS

🏕 Picnic Area

Spencer Butte ▲

P Parking

25

🚰 Drinking Water

🚻 Restrooms

To Cougar

To Cougar

▲ Peaks

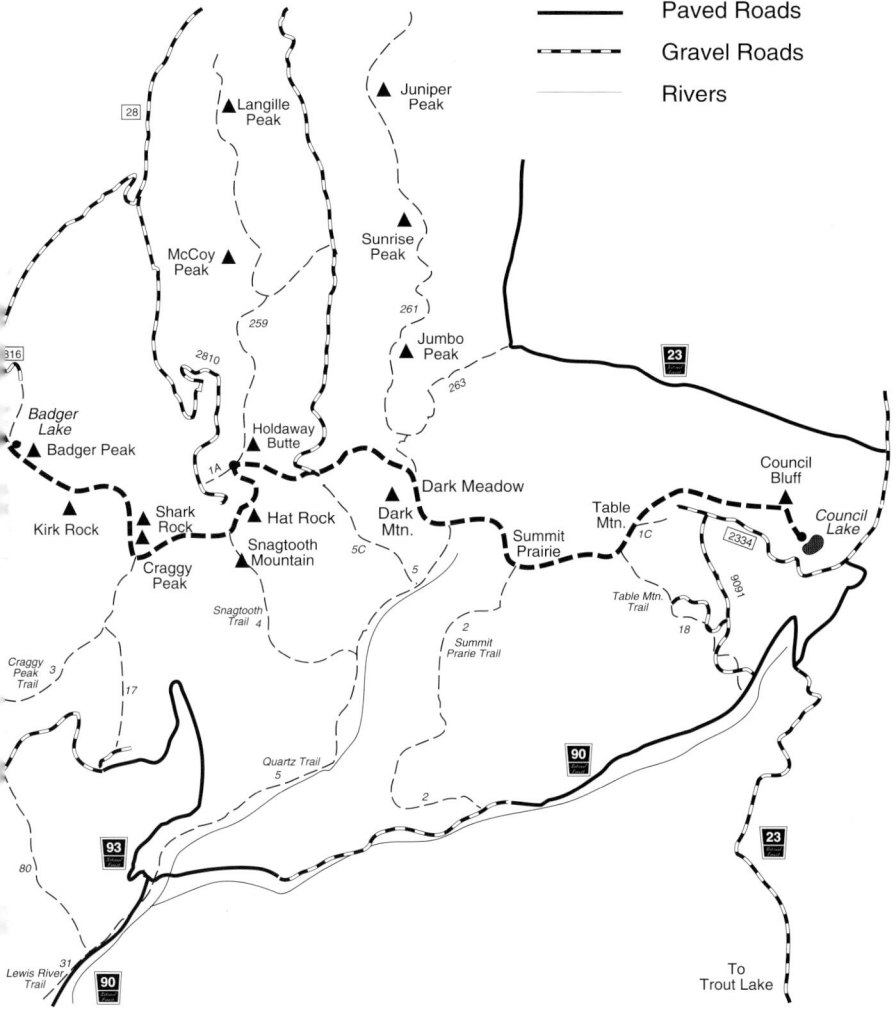

Scale 1/4" = 1mile

N

▬ ▬ ▬ ▬	Main Trail
- - - - -	Connecting Trail
·········	Planned Trail
┿━┿━┿━┿━┿	Restricted Area Trail
▬▬▬▬▬	Paved Roads
▬ ▬ ▬ ▬	Gravel Roads
─────	Rivers

▲ Langille Peak

▲ Juniper Peak

28

McCoy ▲ Peak

▲ Sunrise Peak

261

259

2810

▲ Jumbo Peak

263

23

316

Badger Lake
▲ Badger Peak

Holdaway ▲ Butte

1A

Council Bluff ▲

Council Lake

▲ Kirk Rock

Shark ▲ Rock

▲ Hat Rock

Dark ▲ Mtn.

Dark Meadow

Table Mtn.

1C

2334

9091

Snagtooth ▲ Mountain

Summit Prairie

5C

▲ Craggy Peak

5

Table Mtn. Trail

Snagtooth Trail 4

2

18

Craggy Peak Trail 3

17

Summit Prarie Trail

Quartz Trail 5

90

2

93

80

2

23

90

31 Lewis River Trail

90

To Trout Lake

Boundary Trail #1

Norway Pass Trailhead to
Truman Trail #207 segment

———— Users ————   Difficulty   ———— Facilities ————

Location: begins, Norway Pass Trailhead, Forest Road 26; ends,
    Truman Trail #207
Length: 13.2 miles (one way)
Elevation: 3640 feet, low point; 5850 feet, high point
Season: midsummer to fall
Use: low

Trail Talk:
• Hike along the ridgetop of Mount Margaret and enjoy views of
  alpine meadows and sparkling lakes.
• Although in the midst of the blast zone, the trail is alive with color. In
  summer, rich greens and the vibrant hues of wildflowers paint the area.
• Enjoy captivating views of Mount St. Helens and Spirit Lake that
  improve at each turn.
• To the north, Mount Whittier rises abruptly from the Coldwater Valley,
  and Mount Rainier's snowy shape glistens on the distant horizon.
• Discover beautiful backcountry lakes shimmering like jade green
  jewels in an ashen gray setting.
• Take the side trip to Coldwater Peak and enjoy an outstanding
  panorama of the beautiful Cascade Mountains and Mount St.
  Helens' dynamic volcanic landscape.

Trail Facts: This maintained trail climbs steadily from the trailhead to
Norway Pass and then switchbacks up to Bear Pass. It then traverses the
Mount Margaret ridgeline. It descends from Mt. Margaret and then
climbs steeply to the Coldwater Peak area and ends at its junction with
Truman Trail #207.

Considerations: Snow remains late in the season on north-facing slopes,
making the trail difficult to locate. After the snow melts, little potable
water is available; be sure to bring your own. The trail gains 3000 feet in
elevation (total ups and downs) making it an extremely strenuous day hike.

The Boundary Trail #1 will eventually continue to Johnston Ridge Observatory near Coldwater Lake. Construction will be completed in 1995.

Connections:
• The Boundary Trail #1 extends east to Council Lake near Mount Adams.
• Independence Pass Trail #227 connects at Norway Pass.
• Side Trail #1G climbs to the summit of Coldwater Peak.
• Harrys Ridge Trail #208 connects with the Boundary Trail at its western end.
• Truman Trail #207 junctions at Boundary Trail #1.
• Coldwater Trail #230 connects with the Boundary Trail #1.

Map: Spirit Lake East and Spirit Lake West quadrangles.

Restricted Area: From Norway Pass to the juwith Coldwater Trail #230, the trail is the restricted area boundary. Off-trail travel and camping is allowed uphill of the trail. Use no-trace and low-impact camping methods. In the restricted area travel is allowed on approved trails only. Off-trail travel and camping are prohibited to protect sensitive natural features and scientific studies. Research permits are required for off-trail travel.

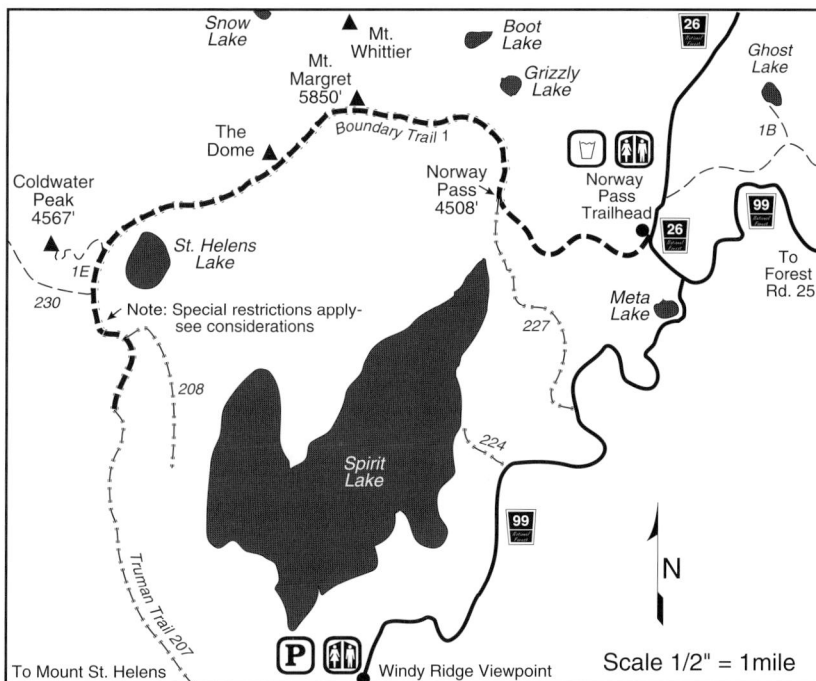

Boundary Trail #1
Norway Pass Trailhead to Norway Pass

———— Users ———— Difficulty ———— Facilities ————

Location: begins, Norway Pass Trailhead, Forest Road 26; ends,
 Norway Pass
Length: 2.2 miles (one way)
Elevation: 3640 feet, low point; 4500 feet, high point
Season: summer to fall
Use: medium

Trail Talk:
• Enjoy one of the Monument's most dramatic views: Mount St.
 Helens' crater and dome reflected in the still blue waters of Spirit
 Lake.
• Scan the skyline for the snowy silhouettes of Mount Adams and
 Mount Rainier.
• Discover avalanche lilies that survived the 1980 eruption and now
 add their graceful beauty to the trail in the summer months.
• Trace the path of the blast as you study the patterns of blown-down
 trees. Along exposed hillsides they were combed into tidy parallel
 lines, but where the blast swirled over ridges they were left in
 tangled messes.
• Look to the east where a formation of ghostly, standing dead trees
 marks the boundary between the blast zone and the adjacent green
 forest.

Trail Facts: This maintained trail climbs to Norway Pass at a steady
grade. It follows the north side of the ridge providing views of Meta
Lake, Mount Adams and Mount Rainier. Mount St. Helens remains
hidden from view until the trail reaches a rewarding vista at Norway
Pass.

Considerations: Portions of the trail are steep and little shade is
offered. Be sure to get water at the trailhead and carry plenty with you.

Connections:

• Norway Pass is a segment of the Boundary Trail system which extends westward through the Mount Margaret backcountry to Truman Trail #207. Eastward, the trail stretches to Council Lake.

• Independence Pass Trail #227 junctions with the Boundary Trail at Norway Pass.

Map: Spirit Lake East quadrangle.

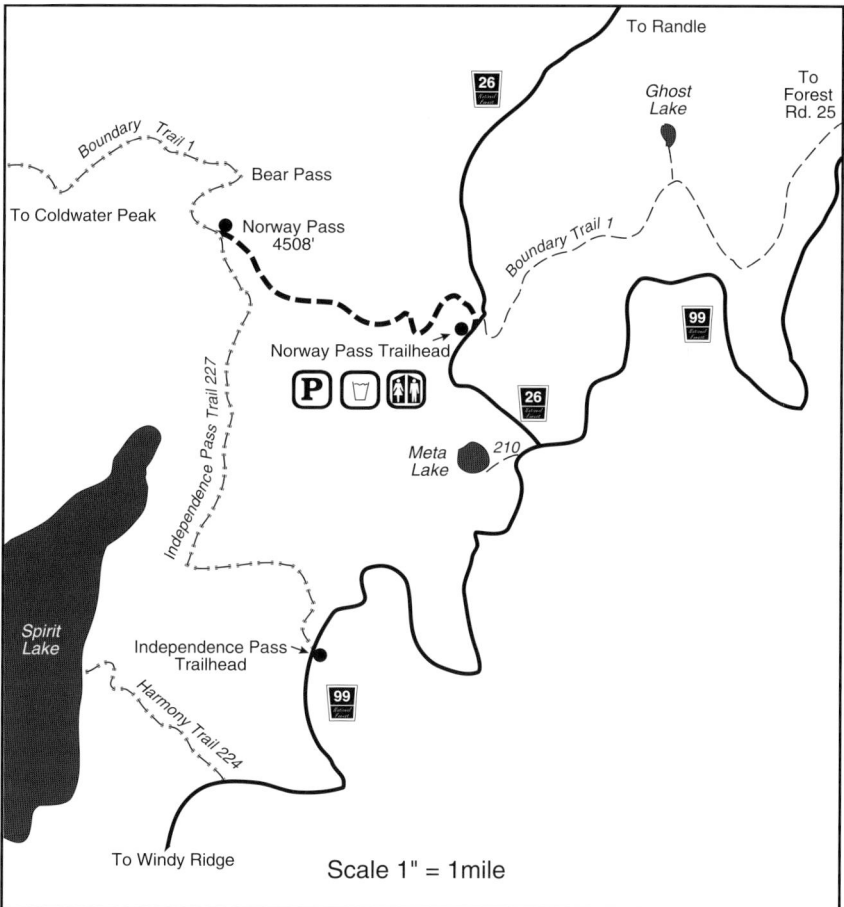

Scale 1" = 1mile

Boundary Trail #1

Norway Pass Trailhead to Elk Pass
Trailhead segment, Ghost Lake Trail #1H

———— Users ———— Difficulty ———— Facilities ————

Location: begins, Norway Pass Trailhead, Forest Road 26; ends, Elk Pass Trailhead, Forest Road 25
Length: 6 miles (one way)
Elevation: 3640 feet, low point; 4520 feet, high point
Season: summer to fall
Use: low

Trail Talk:
• Enjoy excellent views of Mount St. Helens as you hike through the blown-down forest.
• Wind in and out of patches of green and standing dead timber. Discover that many trees were protected from the searing blast winds by high ridges deflecting the main force of the blast, leaving some trees only singed and others untouched.
• Take a side trip to explore the eerie shores of Ghost Lake (Trail #1H). The lake is surrounded by the gray skeletal remains of what was once a lush green forest.
• Notice the small trees that survived the eruption because they were shielded beneath a blanket of snow.
• Catch a glimpse of the past as you enter a forest that is much like the one that once surrounded Mount St. Helens and Spirit Lake.
• Enjoy views of the jagged peak of Mount Hood and the lush young forest of the Clearwater Valley. This valley was salvaged and replanted following the eruption.

Trail Facts: This maintained trail ascends through the blown-down forest. It passes near the Bear Meadow viewpoint and enters the green forest. The section ends at the junction with Forest Road 25. See the next segment for the continuation of Boundary Trail #1 (Elk Pass to Hat Rock segment).

Considerations: Care should be taken not to disturb developing plant and animal life along the fragile shoreline of Ghost Lake. Water is available at Norway Pass Trailhead.

Connections:
• Boundary Trail #1 continues on eastward to Council Lake and westward to Truman Trail #207.
• Trail #1H provides access to Ghost Lake.

Map: Spirit Lake East, French Butte quadrangles.

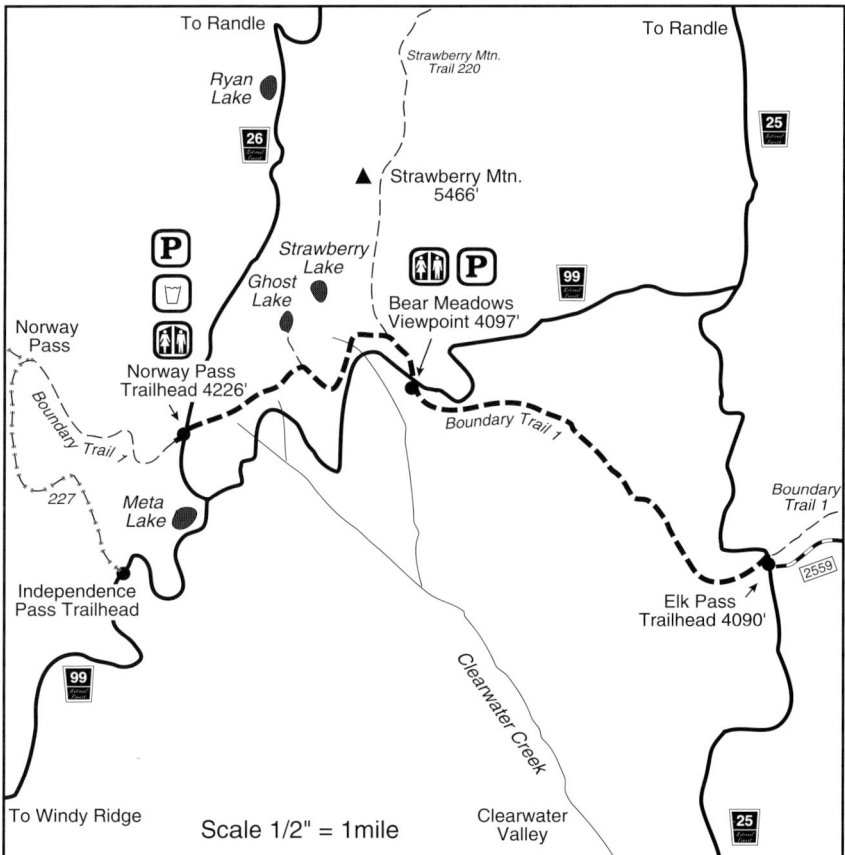

Boundary Trail #1

Elk Pass Trailhead to
Yellowjacket Trail #1A segment

———— Users ————   Difficulty   ——— Facilities ———

Location: begins, Elk Pass Trailhead, Forest Road 25; ends, Hat
   Rock (accessed by Yellowjacket Trail #1A , Forest Road 2810)
Length: 8 miles (one way)
Elevation: 4090 feet, low point; 5000 feet, high point
Season: summer to fall
Use: low

Trail Talk:
- Catch glimpses of Mount Rainier, Pinto Rock and vistas to the south
  as you travel along a ridgetop cloaked in a fir forest.
- At approximately 4 miles, explore a short but rugged side trail (#257)
  to Badger Peak. The view from the summit is superb. A Forest
  Service fire lookout cabin was once perched on top of this rocky
  peak.
- Take a refreshing break at Badger Lake where a pumice beach, cool
  waters and green meadows await you.
- Follow the ridge through a canopy of trees until you break out into
  the open near the towering walls of Kirk Rock. Marmots inhabit
  the area so listen for their shrill whistles of alarm.
- Alternating views to the north and south await you as you make your
  way towards the pinnacle of Shark Rock.
- Beneath the crown of Craggy Peak is the junction of Craggy Peak
  Trail #3.
- Descend to Yellowjacket Pass and then climb through the forest
  until passing beneath the impressive cliffs of Hat Rock.
- The summit of Craggy Peak can be reached by following a climbers'
  path up the south ridge, leave the Boundary Trail at the high point
  where the trail crosses the saddle just east of the Craggy Peak Trail
  junction.

Trail Facts: This maintained trail travels at a fairly level grade until Shark Rock. East of Shark Rock the trail makes a series of steep ascents and descents before junctioning with Yellowjacket Trail #1A (accessed on Forest Road 2810).

Considerations: The 1980 Mount St. Helens eruption cloud deposited a thick layer of pumice on the trail, making hiking and mountain biking difficult. Water is available but should be treated before drinking.

Connections:
• Boundary Trail #1 continues to both the east and west. A side trail (#257) climbs to the summit of Badger Peak.
• Trail #292 exits out to Mosquito Meadows on Forest Road 28.
• Near Craggy Peak, Trail #3 heads south.
• Near Hat Rock, Yellowjacket Trail #1A exits to Forest Road 2810.

Map: French Butte and McCoy quadrangles.

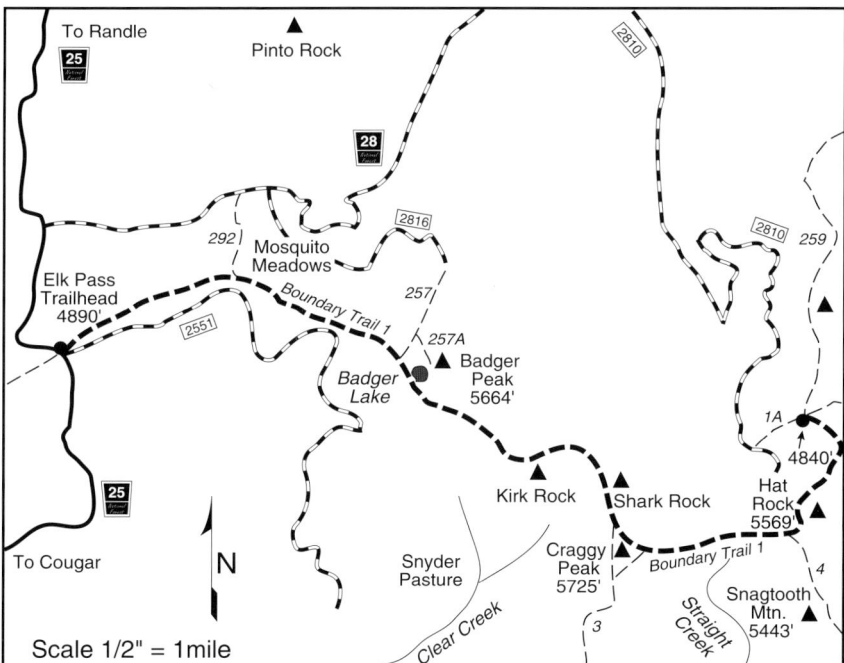

Boundary Trail #1
Yellowjacket Trail #1A to
Council Lake segment

———— Users ————   Difficulty   ———— Facilities ————

Location: begins, Yellowjacket Trail #1A, Forest Road 2810; ends,
   Council Lake, Forest Road 2334
Length: 13.8 miles (one way)
Elevation: 5283 feet, high point; 4221 feet, low point
Season: midsummer to fall
Use: low

Trail Talk:
• Obtain expansive views of the South Cascade Mountains.
• Enjoy emerald-green Dark Mountain meadows.
• Pass beneath the flat plateau of Table Mountain.
• Find solitude in this remote setting.
• Access numerous scenic trails and enjoy extended loop opportunities.

Trail Facts: This maintained trail travels along the divide of the
Lewis and Cispus River watersheds. Its elevation is 4000 feet or above,
ascending and descending out of stream drainages.

Considerations: Preserve the high country beauty of this area by
following low-impact camping and user methods.

Connections:
• Langille Ridge Trail #259 heads north to Holdaway Butte and out
  onto Langille Ridge, and McCoy Peak.
• Juniper Peak Trail #261 goes to Jumbo Peak, Sunrise Peak and
  Juniper Peak.
• Quartz Creek Trail #5 heads south to Forest Road 90.
• Summit Prairie Trail #2 heads south to Forest Road 90.
• Table Mountain Trail #18 heads south to Forest Road 90.
• Near Council Lake, Council Bluff Trail #117 climbs to the Bluff's
  summit.

Map: McCoy Peak and East Canyon Ridge quadrangles.

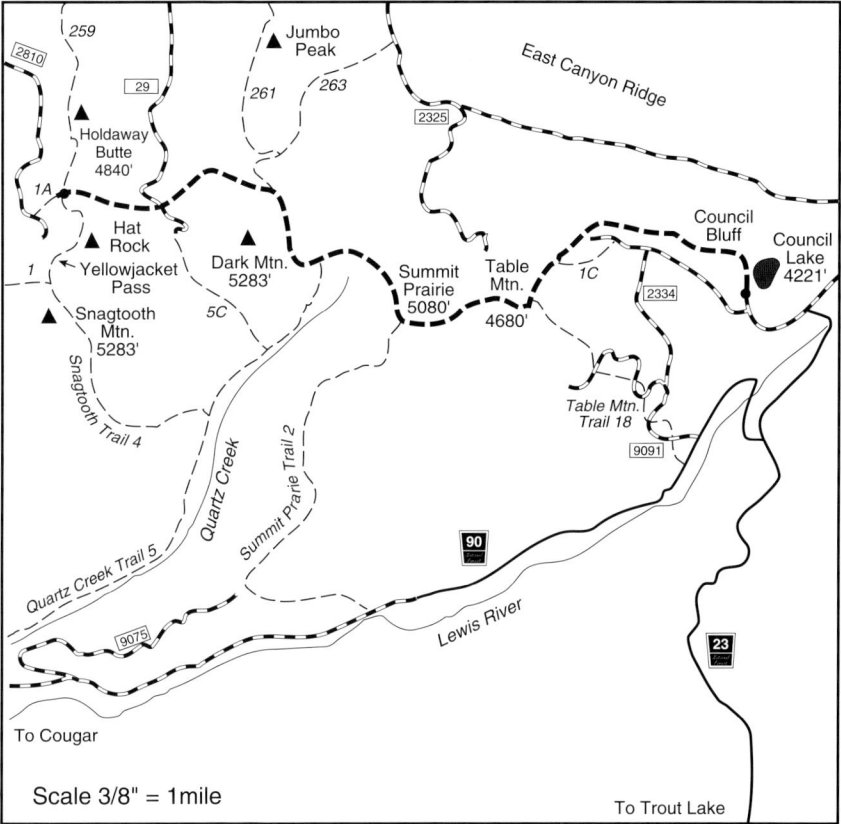

259
2810
29
Jumbo Peak
261 263
East Canyon Ridge
2325
Holdaway Butte 4840'
1A
Hat Rock
Council Bluff
Council Lake 4221'
1
Yellowjacket Pass
Dark Mtn. 5283'
Summit Prairie 5080'
Table Mtn.
1C
Snagtooth Mtn. 5283'
5C
Table Mtn. 4680'
2334
Snagtooth Trail 4
Quartz Creek
Summit Prarie Trail 2
Table Mtn. Trail 18
9091
Quartz Creek Trail 5
90
9075
Lewis River
23
To Cougar
Scale 3/8" = 1mile
To Trout Lake

Summit Prairie Trail #2

———— Users ———— Difficulty ——— Facilities ————

Location: begins, Forest Road 90; ends, Boundary Trail #1
Length: 9 miles (one way)
Elevation: 2400 feet, low point; 5240 feet, high point
Season: summer to fall
Use: low

Trail Talk:
• Take an invigorating uphill hike through forest slopes and be
  rewarded with impressive views as you near the summit of Quartz
  Creek Ridge.
• Meander along the ridgetop through alpine forests and high country
  meadows as you enjoy the views of the tree-lined valleys of Quartz
  and French creeks.
• Scan the horizon for outstanding panoramas filled with snowcapped
  volcanoes and the high open ridges of the Dark Divide Roadless
  Area.
• Discover the remains of the Summit Prairie fire lookout which was
  built in 1932.
• Hike to the junction of Boundary Trail #1 where a small prairie was
  previously a grazing spot for sheep herds that once roamed these
  hillsides.

Trail Facts: This maintained trail climbs steeply through the forest for
2 miles, crosses Road 9075 and continues on to Quartz Creek Ridge. It
then traverses an open to semi-open ridgetop for 4 miles before climbing to the old Summit Prairie Lookout.

Considerations: No water is available beyond the first section of the
trail. A sign along Forest Road 90 marks the beginning of the trail.

Connections:

• The trail connects with the Boundary Trail #1 system, near Table Mountain Trail #18.
• Loop opportunities are available by using Quartz Creek Trail #5 or Table Mtn. Trail #18. Both begin on Road 90.

Map: Steamboat Mtn. and East Canyon Ridge quadrangles.

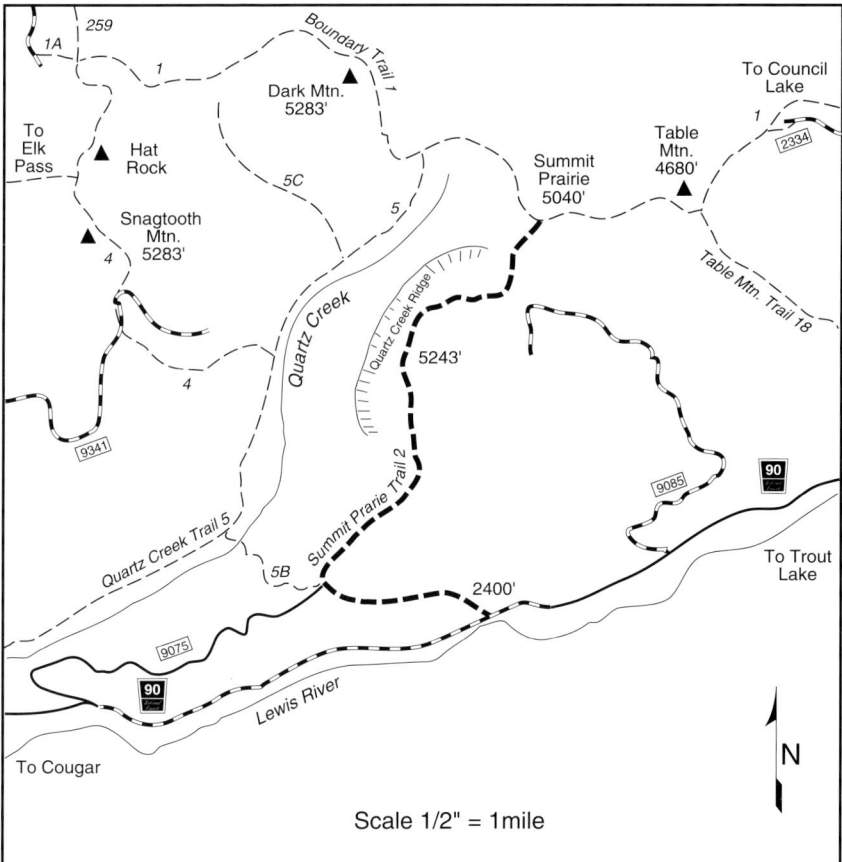

Scale 1/2" = 1mile

Craggy Peak Trail #3

———— Users ———— Difficulty ———— Facilities ————

Location: begins, Forest Road 9327-040 spur; ends, Boundary
   Trail #1
Length: 4.4 miles (one way)
Elevation: 3600 feet, low point; 5200 feet, high point
Season: summer to fall
Use: low

Trail Talk:
• Travel along a ridge top beneath the deep green canopy of a Pacific
  silver and noble fir forest.
• Catch peek-a-boo views of Mount Rainier and the impressive rock
  formations of the Shark Rock Area (see Boundary Trail #1).
• Search the east side of the trail and discover Blue Lake's shimmer-
  ing surface almost 400 feet below.
• Enter emerald meadows and enjoy the summer display of subalpine
  wildflowers.
• Gaze across the rolling carpet of green forest that extends to the foot
  of Mount Adams.
• Watch for the side trail to Basin Camp, a good place to camp for
  stunning sunrise and sunset views of Mount Adams.
• Pass Basin Camp pond where elk and deer wallow to rid themselves
  of flies and insects.
• Connect into the Boundary Trail #1 near the crown of Craggy Peak.

Trail Facts: This maintained trail climbs gently along a forested
ridge. As it gains in elevation it becomes steeper and the views are
more open. Blue Lake is sighted far below the trail as the first small
subalpine meadow is reached. Side trails to campsites can be found.
The trail connects with Boundary Trail #1 near Craggy Peak.

Considerations: Water can be scarce after the snow melts. The fragile meadows are easily damaged by misuse. Please adhere to low-impact, backcountry use ethics to preserve the beauty of this area.

Connections:
• Craggy Peak Trail #3 connects with Wright Meadow Trail #80 to the south.
• At its north end, it junctions with Boundary Trail #1.

Map: Spencer Butte, Quartz Creek Butte, and McCoy Peak quadrangles.

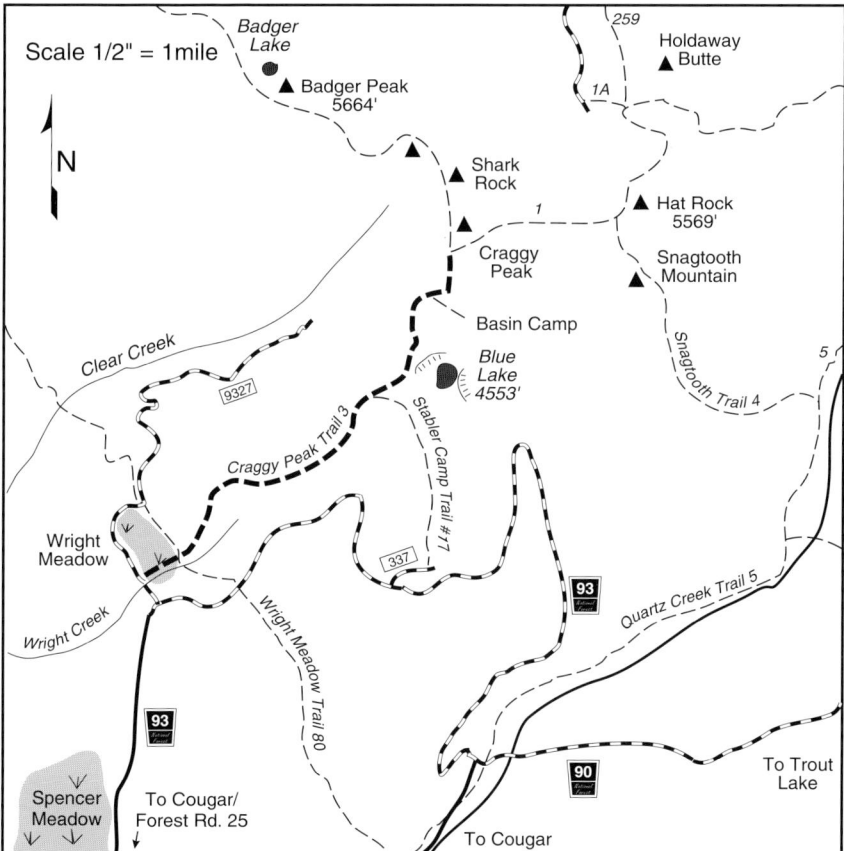

Snagtooth Trail #4

————— Users —————   Difficulty   ————— Facilities —————

Location: begins, Quartz Creek Trail #5; ends, Boundary Trail #1
Length: 4.8 miles (one way)
Elevation: 2600 feet, low point; 5000 feet, high point
Season: summer to fall
Use: low

Trail Talk:
• Climb through a managed forest.
• Enjoy views of the French Creek basin.
• Pass below the rocky summit of Snagtooth Mountain.
• Gain quick access to the Boundary Trail #1 near Yellowjacket Pass.

Trail Facts: This maintained trail climbs steeply from Quartz Creek Trail to its connection with Boundary Trail #1 near Yellowjacket Pass. The trail can also be accessed on Road 9341 for a shorter but steep route to the Boundary Trail.

Considerations: This steep trail is used for rapid access to both the Quartz Creek Trail #5 and the Boundary Trail #1.

Connections:
• Snagtooth Trail #4 forms a connection between the Quartz Creek Trail and the Boundary Trail.

Map: McCoy Peak and Quartz Creek quadrangle.

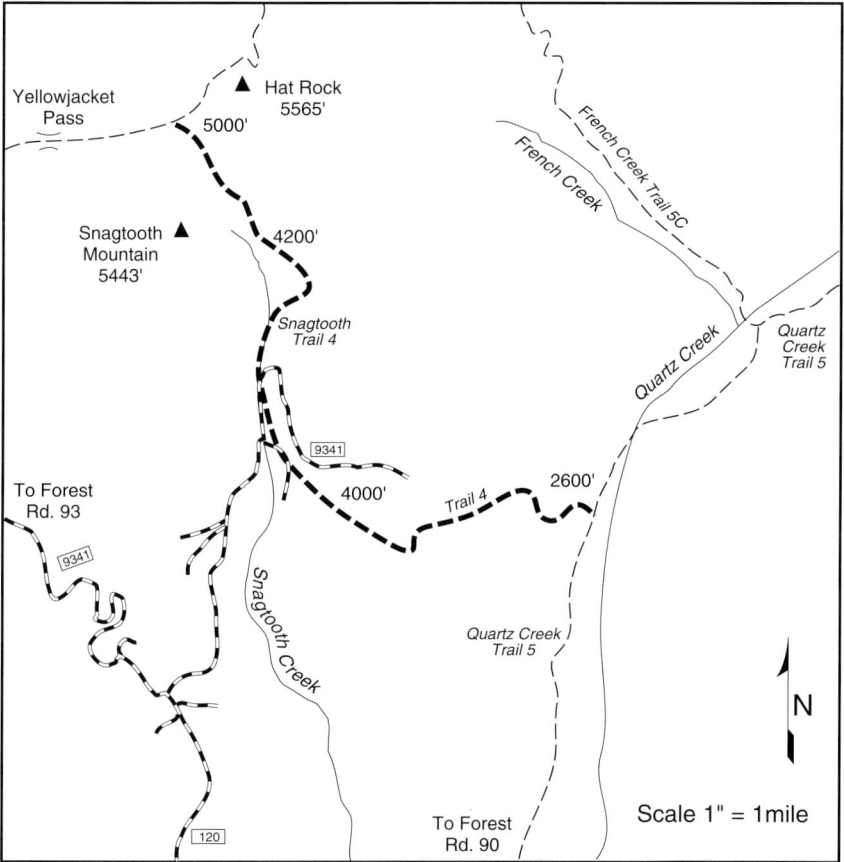

Yellowjacket Pass

Hat Rock 5565'

5000'

Snagtooth Mountain 5443'

4200'

Snagtooth Trail 4

9341

4000'

To Forest Rd. 93

9341

Snagtooth Creek

Trail 4

2600'

French Creek

French Creek Trail 5C

Quartz Creek

Quartz Creek Trail 5

Quartz Creek Trail 5

120

To Forest Rd. 90

N

Scale 1" = 1mile

Quartz Creek Trail #5

——— Users ——— Difficulty ——— Facilities ———

Location: begins, Quartz Creek Trailhead, Forest Road 90; ends,
   Boundary Trail #1
Length: 10.6 miles (one way)
Elevation: 1800 feet, low point; 4200 feet, high point
Season: summer to fall
Use: low

Trail Talk:
• Discover an ancient forest of magnificent cedars, firs and hemlocks.
• Hike along Quartz Creek Canyon whose walls are lined with old-
  growth trees, and cliff faces are blanketed with mosses and ferns.
• Follow the canyon's edge and look down on the crystal clear
  stream as it flows over color-streaked bedrock, pauses in pools, and
  plunges over waterfalls.
• Explore the numerous side streams that flow into Quartz Creek. Discover a series of waterfalls along Straight Creek.
• Enjoy primitive campsites within the sight and sound of cascading
  water.
• See the effects of wildfire. It transformed the once lushly forested
  upper valley of Quartz Creek into its current subalpine appearance.
• Discover craggy spires of exposed rock and steep rocky slopes as
  you break out into the upper section of the Quartz Creek Trail.

Trail Facts: This trail follows Quartz Creek drainage, although access
to the stream is limited. It is a steep trail (43% grade), ascending and
descending through numerous side drainages as it climbs its way up the
valley.

Considerations: The trail is steep over long sections. It is scheduled
for reconstruction during 1994 and 1995. Following reconstruction, the
trail will offer more camping opportunities, scenic views, and a reduced

difficulty standard as well as enhanced access to Quartz Creek. A steep rock side slope near French Creek is dangerous or impossible for horses to pass. Check with Monument Headquarters for current trail conditions.

Connections:

• Quartz Creek Trail #5 junctions with the Lewis River Trail #31 across Forest Road 90.
• Quartz Butte Trail #5B connects Quartz Creek Trail to Summit Prairie Trail #2.
• The French Creek Trail #5C used to connect the Quartz Creek Trail to Boundary Trail #1 near the upper end. Reconstruction in 1994/95 will restore it.

Map: Quartz Creek Butte, East Canyon Ridge, and McCoy Peak quadrangles.

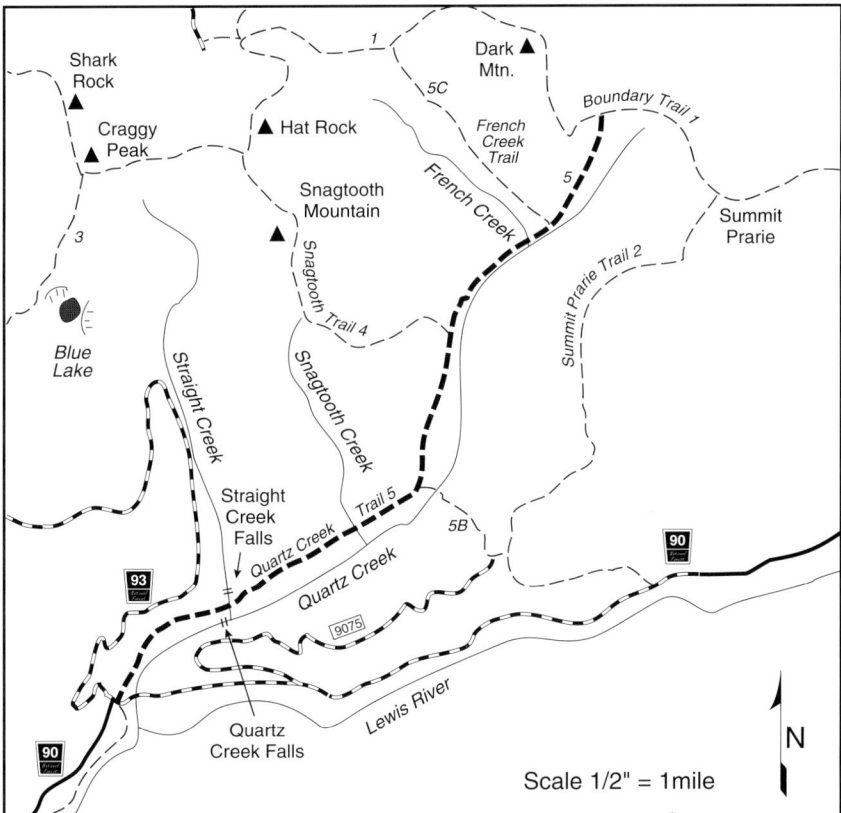

Quartz Creek Butte Trail #5B

———— Users ———— Difficulty ———— Facilities ————

Location: begins, Summit Prairie Trail #2; ends, Quartz Creek
  Trail #5
Length: 1.5 miles (one way)
Elevation: 3600 feet, high point; 2200 feet, low point
Season: summer to fall
Use: low

Trail Talk:
• Enjoy a long-distance backpacking opportunity by using this trail to
  access the Summit Prairie Trail #2 from the Quartz Creek Trail #5.
• Pass through a mature stand of Douglas-fir and Pacific silver fir
  trees.
• Find solitude in this remote setting.

Trail Facts: This maintained trail makes a steep descent through a
forested area from Summit Prairie Trail #2 to Quartz Creek Trail #5.

Considerations: The first 1/3 mile climbing out of the Quartz Creek
drainage is the steepest portion of the trail.

Connections:
• Quartz Creek Butte Trail #5B connects Quartz Creek Trail #5 and
  Summit Prairie Trail #2.

Map: Quartz Creek Butte quadrangle.

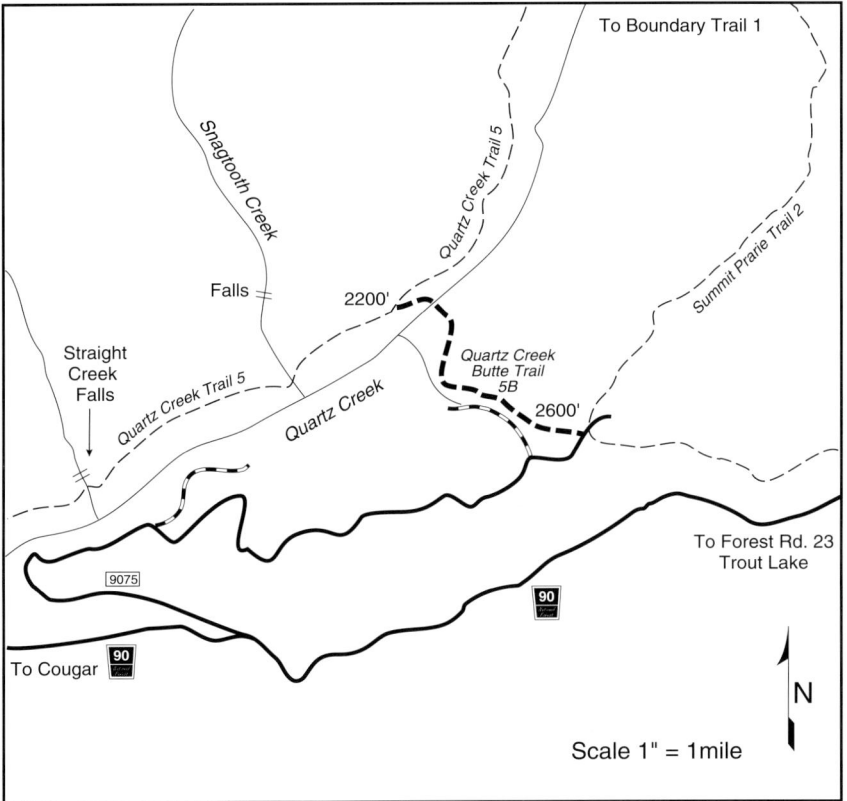

To Boundary Trail 1

Snagtooth Creek

Quartz Creek Trail 5

Summit Prarie Trail 2

Falls

2200'

Quartz Creek Butte Trail 5B

2600'

Straight Creek Falls

Quartz Creek Trail 5

Quartz Creek

9075

90

To Forest Rd. 23
Trout Lake

To Cougar 90

N

Scale 1" = 1mile

French Creek Trail #5C

——— Users ———   Difficulty   ——— Facilities ———

Location: begins, upper portion of Quartz Creek Trail #5; ends, Boundary Trail #1
Length: 3.25 miles (one way)
Elevation: 3040 feet, low point; 3750 feet, high point
Season: summer to fall
Use: low

Trail Talk:
• Travel along the forested drainage of French Creek.
• Find solitude in this remote setting.
• Discover the evidence of past fires. Note the small size of the trees and the silver, twisted shapes of old snags.
• Enjoy the views available through the openings along the trail.

Trail Facts: This is an unmaintained trail following the French Creek drainage. It connects Quartz Creek Trail #5 to Boundary Trail #1 (see considerations). It's accessed from the Quartz Creek Trail.

Considerations: The trail is unsigned and difficult to follow. A contour map and orienteering skills are recommended. When reconstruction is complete, trail difficulty rating will be changed.

Connections:
• Reconstruction in 1994/95 will reopen the connection of French Creek Trail #5C to Boundary Trail #1.

Map: McCoy Peak quadrangle.

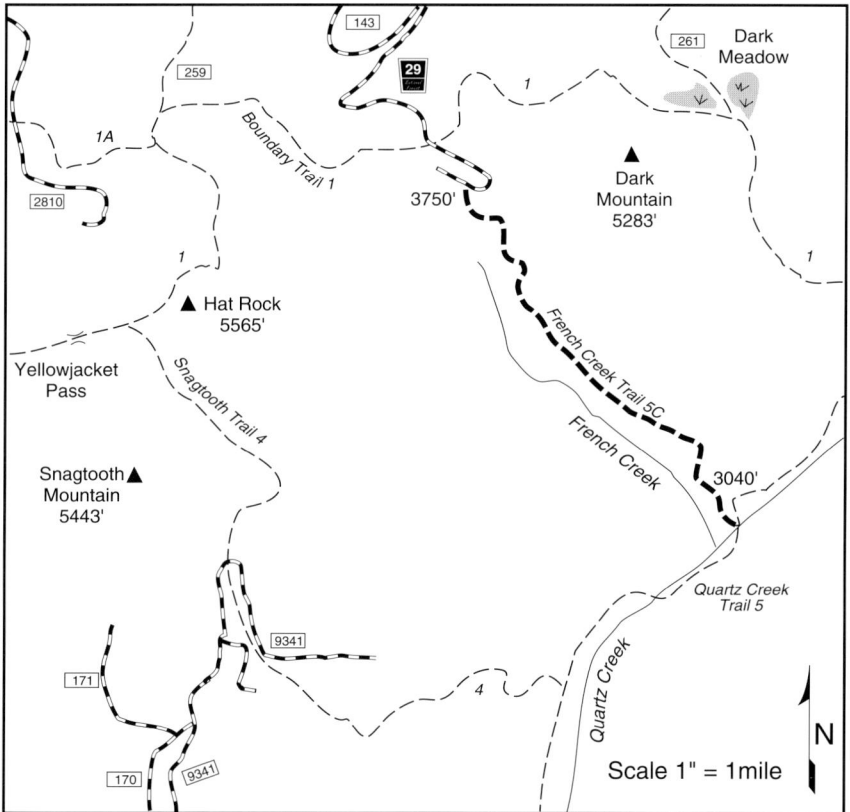

143

259

29

261 Dark Meadow

1A

1

Boundary Trail 1

2810

3750'

Dark Mountain 5283'

▲

1

1

▲ Hat Rock 5565'

French Creek Trail 5C

Yellowjacket Pass

Snagtooth Trail 4

French Creek

3040'

Snagtooth▲ Mountain 5443'

Quartz Creek Trail 5

9341

Quartz Creek

171

4

170 9341

Scale 1" = 1mile

N

House Rock Trail #6

———— Users ———— Difficulty ———— Facilities ————

Location: begins, 240 spur off Forest Road 9310; ends, House Rock Shelter
Length: 0.5 mile
Elevation: 2400 feet
Season: spring to late fall
Use: low

Trail Talk:
• This short trail meanders through a young forest with views of nearby forests.
• Hike to a newly reconstructed cedar shelter at House Rock, with spectacular views overlooking the Lewis River valley and Mount St. Helens.

Trail Facts: The trail begins in a clearcut at the end of the 240 spur off Road 9310. It climbs at an easy grade through a medium-age forest to the shelter on a bluff on House Rock.

Considerations: Roads leading to the trail are primitive and not well maintained.

Connections:
• The trail ends at the House Rock Shelter.

Map: Burnt Peak quadrangle.

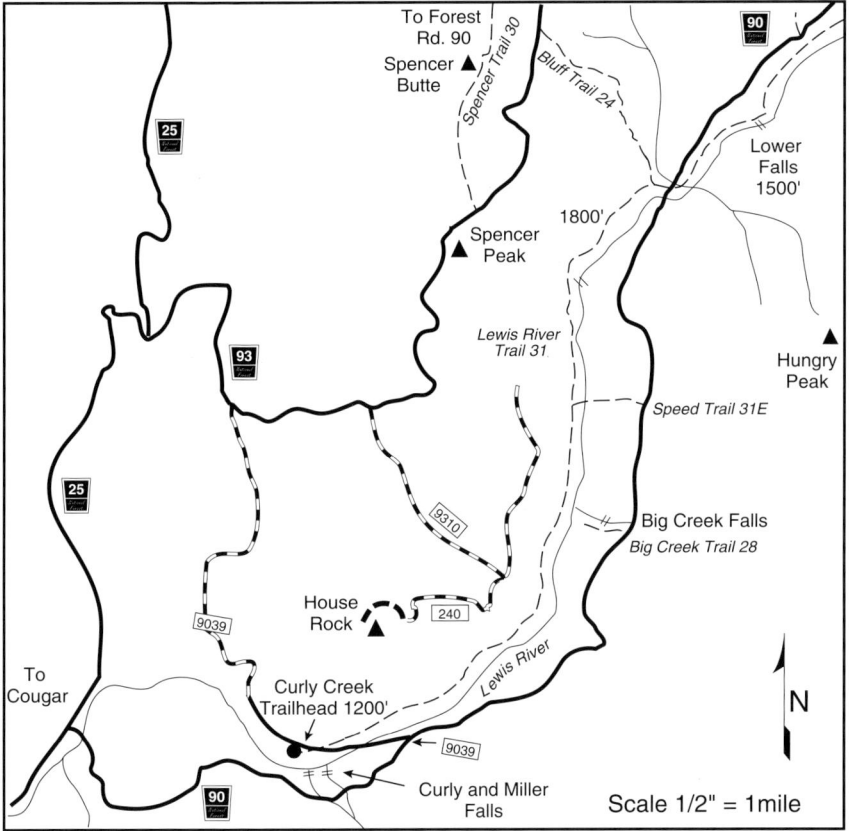

To Forest Rd. 90

Spencer Butte ▲

Spencer Trail 30

Bluff Trail 24

90

Lower Falls 1500'

25

Spencer Peak ▲

1800'

Lewis River Trail 31

Hungry Peak ▲

93

Speed Trail 31E

25

9310

Big Creek Falls

Big Creek Trail 28

House Rock ▲

240

9039

Lewis River

To Cougar

Curly Creek Trailhead 1200'

9039

N

90

Curly and Miller Falls

Scale 1/2" = 1mile

Stabler Camp #17

——— Users ——— Difficulty ——— Facilities ———

Location: begins, spur 337 off Forest Road 93; ends, junction with Craggy Peak Trail
Length: 2.6 miles (one way)
Elevation: 4000 feet, low point; 4600 feet, high point
Season: late spring to fall
Use: low

Trail Talk:
• This intermittently maintained trail provides a secluded high country hiking or riding opportunity.
• Enjoy alpine meadows and forests with meandering streams.
• Catch glimpses of elk and other wildlife.

Trail Facts: The trail begins in a clearcut near the end of the 9337 spur road. It climbs gradually through an alpine forest and levels off through a series of small meadows. It passes through a recent clearcut and then climbs through more forest before crossing a gravel road (Road 9331, closed to motorized use). The trail then climbs for another 1/4 mile to the junction with Craggy Peak Trail #3.

Considerations: This trail is intermittently maintained–obstacles and brushy conditions may be encountered. The trail crosses Road 9331 which leads to the Blue Lake area, but this road is closed to motor vehicles.

Connections: The trail connects with Craggy Peak Trail #3.

Map: Quartz Creek Butte quadrangle.

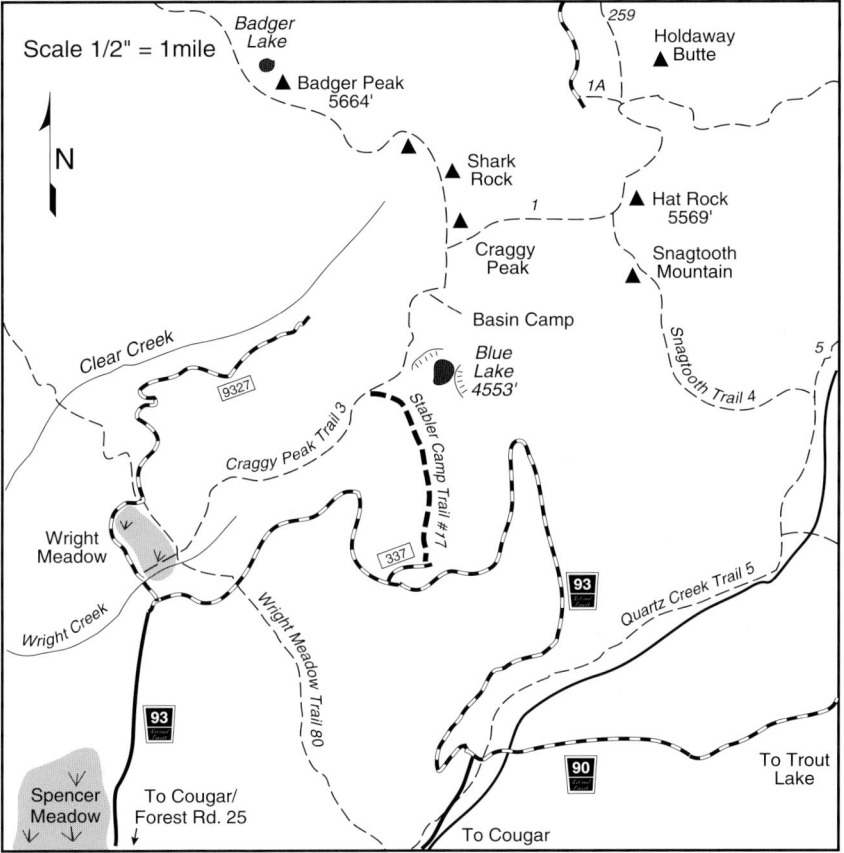

Scale 1/2" = 1mile

N

Badger Lake

259

Holdaway
▲ Butte

▲ Badger Peak
5664'

1A

▲ Shark
Rock

1

▲ Hat Rock
5569'

▲ Craggy
Peak

▲ Snagtooth
Mountain

Basin Camp

Blue Lake
4553'

Clear Creek

9327

Snagtooth Trail 4

5

Craggy Peak Trail 3

Stabler Camp Trail #17

Wright
Meadow

337

93

Wright Creek

Quartz Creek Trail 5

Wright Meadow Trail 80

93

90

To Trout
Lake

Spencer
Meadow

To Cougar/
Forest Rd. 25

To Cougar

Table Mountain Trail #18

——— Users ———   Difficulty   ——— Facilities ———

Location: begins, Forest Road 90; ends, Boundary Trail #1
Length: 5 miles (one way)
Elevation: 3080 feet, low point; 4680 feet, high point
Season: midsummer to fall
Use: low

Trail Talk:
• Hike through a forest setting.
• Discover numerous ponds surrounded by grassy meadows.
• Wildlife viewing opportunities abound.

Trail Facts: This maintained trail climbs steadily through the forest. At the northern end it enters meadows and passes by numerous ponds. It then junctions with Boundary Trail #1.

Considerations: The trail is crossed numerous times by Forest Road 9095. Water is available but must be treated for safe drinking. Meadow areas are fragile; please take care, and use low-impact camping and hiking methods.

Connections:
• Table Mountain Trail #18 connects with Boundary Trail #1 at its northern end.

Map: Steamboat Mountain and East Canyon Ridge quadrangles.

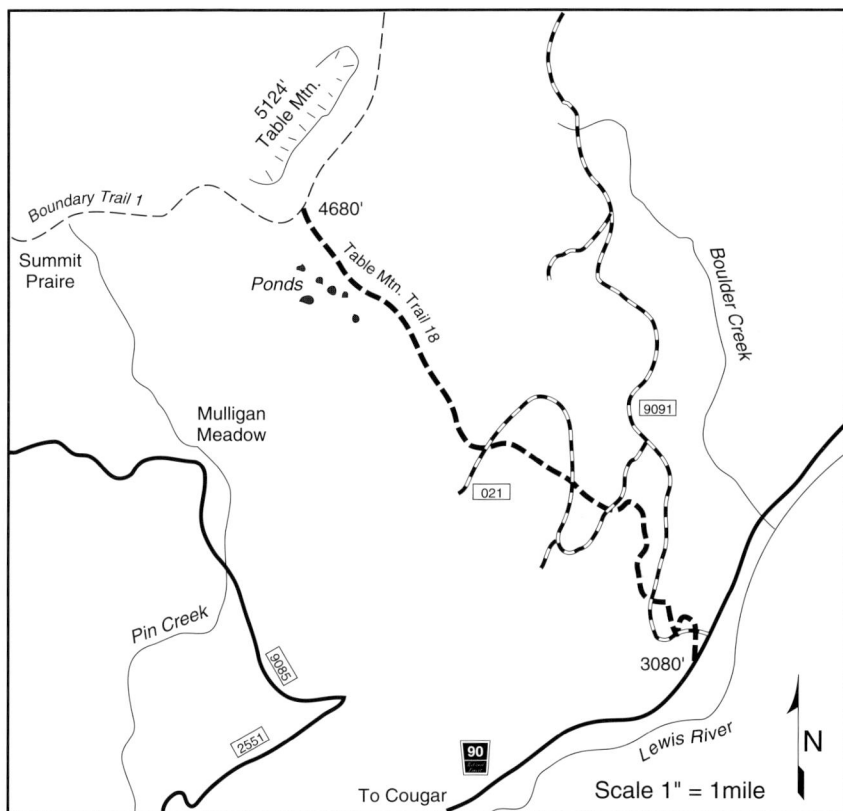

Boundary Trail 1

5124'
Table Mtn.

4680'

Summit
Praire

Ponds

Table Mtn. Trail 18

Boulder Creek

Mulligan
Meadow

9091

021

Pin Creek

9085

3080'

2551

90

To Cougar

Lewis River

Scale 1" = 1mile

N

Cussed Hollow Trail #19

———— Users ———— Difficulty ———— Facilities ————

Location: begins, Forest Road 93; ends, Wright Meadow Trail #80
Length: 3.3 miles (one way)
Elevation: 3420 feet, high point; 2420 feet, low point
Season: late spring to fall
Use: low

Trail Talk:
• Pass through a western white pine forest and as you descend in elevation, enter into a stand of stately Douglas-fir and Pacific silver fir trees.
• This trail is very popular with horse users.
• Views along the trail are obscured by the dense and many-layered canopy.

Trail Facts: This maintained trail descends at a steep and steady grade. It follows along the course of Cussed Hollow Creek and then passes through an old burn area near the junction of the Wright Meadow Trail. From there it is approximately 3/4 mile via Wright Meadow Trail #80 to Forest Road 90.

Considerations: Water for stock is available at the ford on Cussed Hollow Creek. Water intended for human consumption should be treated for safe drinking.

Connections:
• The Cussed Hollow Trail connects with Wright Meadow Trail #80.

Map: Spencer Butte quadrangle.

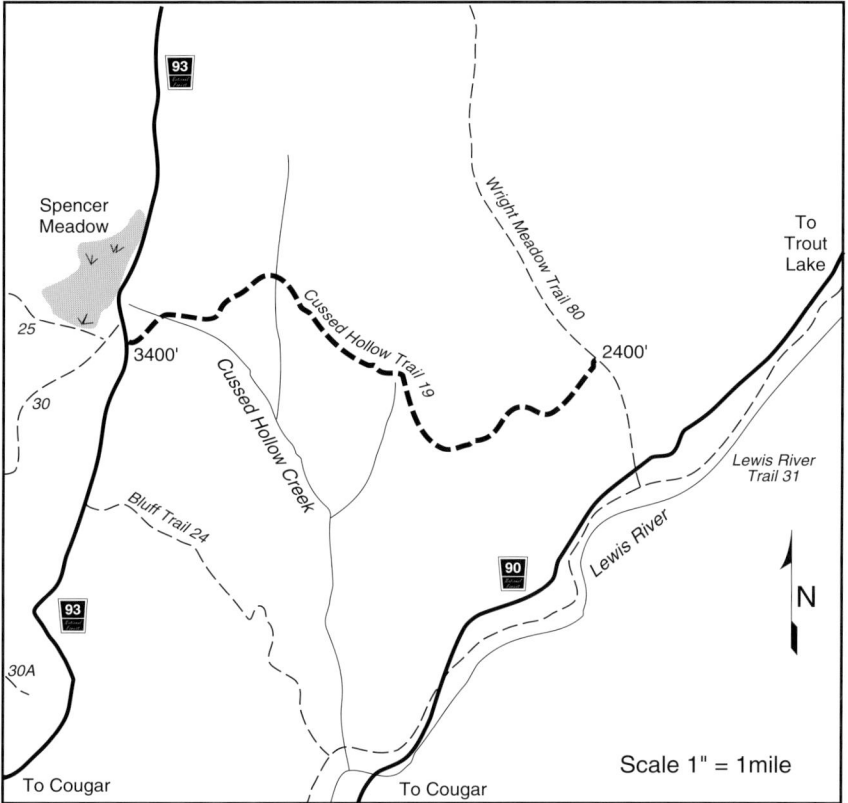

93

Spencer
Meadow

25

3400'

30

Cussed Hollow Creek

Cussed Hollow Trail 19

Wright Meadow Trail 80

2400'

To
Trout
Lake

Lewis River
Trail 31

Bluff Trail 24

Lewis River

90

93

30A

N

To Cougar

To Cougar

Scale 1" = 1mile

Bluff Trail #24

————— Users ————— Difficulty ————— Facilities —————

Location: begins, Forest Road 93; ends, Lewis River Trail #31
Length: 2.7 miles (one way)
Elevation: 3440 feet, high point; 1560 feet, low point
Season: early summer to fall
Use: low

Trail Talk:
• Enjoy an exceptional view of Mount Adams and the Lewis River
  Valley at the trailhead.
• Pass through a second-growth Douglas-fir forest that regenerated
  after the Spencer Burn.
• The trail was used as an old "way" trail (quickest way) to reach the
  Lewis River from Spencer Butte Lookout before roads were built in
  the area.

Trail Facts: This maintained trail loses 2000 feet in elevation as it
descends to the Lewis River. It traverses down a ridgeline and connects
into Lewis River Trail #31 near Cussed Hollow Creek, about 1/4 mile
downstream from the upper bridge crossing of the Lewis River on
Forest Road 90.

Considerations: Water is unavailable until you near the vicinity of
the Lewis River. All water should be treated for safe drinking.

Connections:
• Connects with Lewis River Trail #31.

Map: Spencer Butte quadrangle.

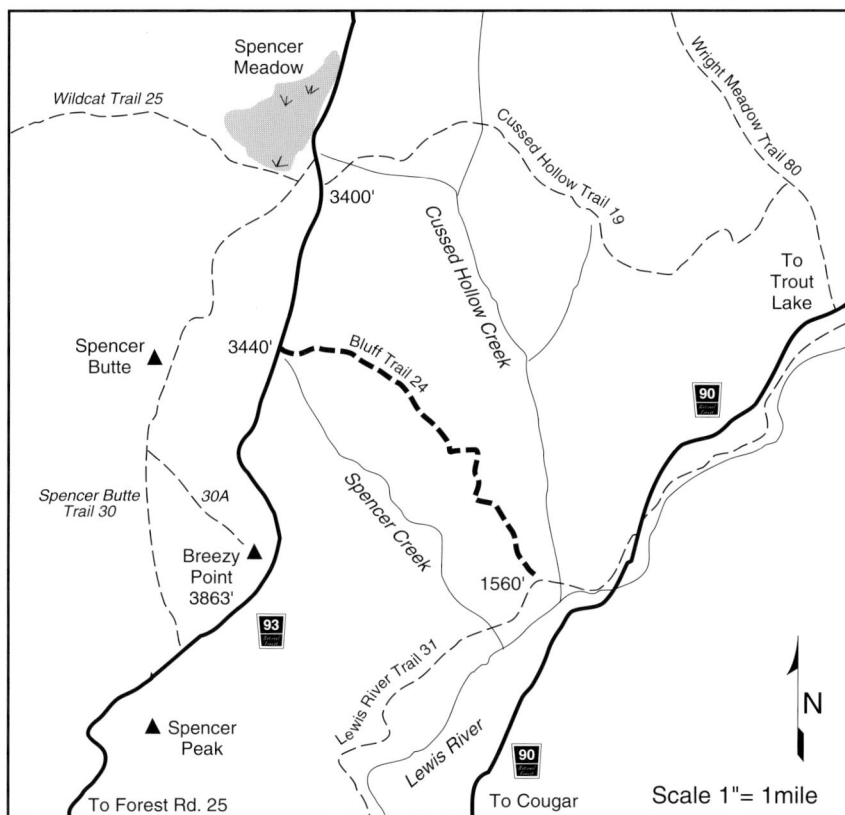

Spencer
Meadow

Wildcat Trail 25

Cussed Hollow Trail 19

Wright Meadow Trail 80

3400'

Cussed Hollow Creek

To
Trout
Lake

Spencer
Butte

3440'

Bluff Trail 24

90

Spencer Butte
Trail 30

30A

Breezy
Point
3863'

Spencer Creek

93

1560'

Spencer
Peak

Lewis River Trail 31

Lewis River

90

To Forest Rd. 25

To Cougar

N

Scale 1"= 1mile

Wildcat Trail #25

Location: begins, Forest Road 93; ends, Forest Road 2573
Length: 4.5 miles (one way)
Elevation: 3400 feet, high point; 1400 feet, low point; 3100 feet,
  high point
Season: early summer to fall
Use: low

Trail Talk:
• Take a side trip to Spencer Meadow to view the elk that are often
  found grazing there.
• Stroll through a western white pine forest and break out into small
  sunlit meadows on the first section of trail.
• After the first 1 1/2 miles, the trail becomes overgrown and starts a
  steep descent toward Clear Creek.
• This historic trail was used in the 1930s to connect Spencer Butte
  lookout to Clear Ridge lookout.

Trail Facts: This unmaintained trail follows a level grade through a
western white pine forest for approximately 1 1/4 miles. It then descends into a Douglas-fir forest at a steep grade and becomes hard to
distinguish.

Considerations: The trail is steep, difficult to follow and is often
crisscrossed by game trails. A compass, topographic map and
orienteering skills are strongly recommended.

Connections:
• No direct connections.

Map: Spencer Butte quadrangle.

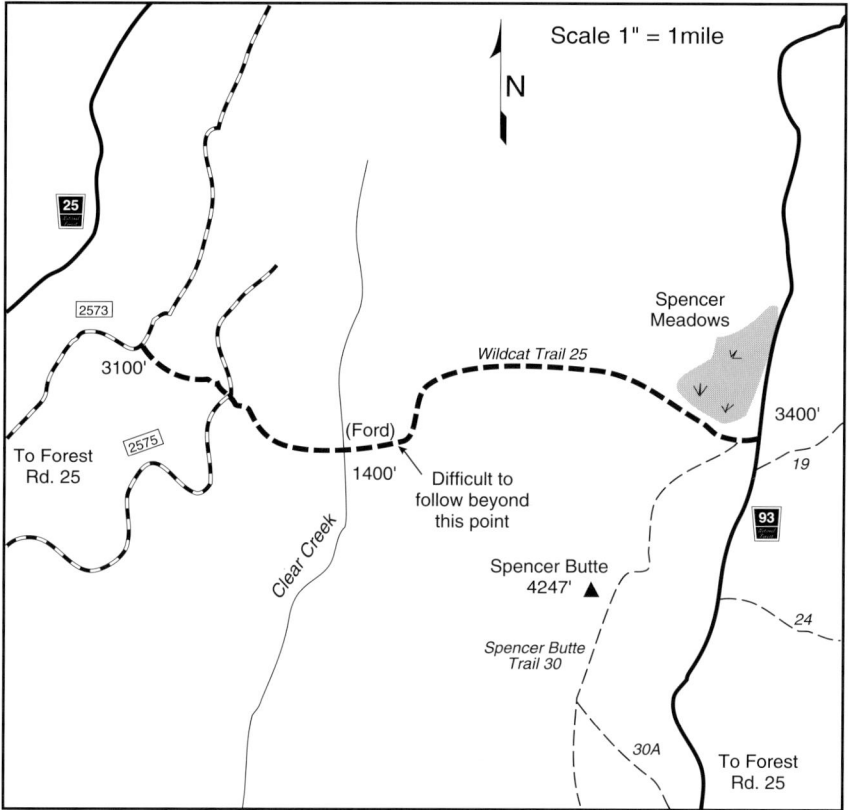

Scale 1" = 1mile

N

25

2573

3100'

To Forest
Rd. 25

2575

(Ford)

1400'

Difficult to
follow beyond
this point

Clear Creek

Wildcat Trail 25

Spencer
Meadows

3400'

19

93

24

Spencer Butte
4247'

Spencer Butte
Trail 30

30A

To Forest
Rd. 25

Big Creek Trail #28

—————— Users —————— Difficulty ——————— Facilities ———————

Location: begins, Big Creek Trailhead, Forest Road 90
Length: Barrier-free loop 0.25 miles
Length: Big Creek Trail 0.7 miles (one way)
Elevation: 2000 feet, high point; 1800 feet, low point
Season: spring to late fall
Use: medium

Trail Talk:
• Become enchanted with breathtaking Big Creek Falls as it plunges
  110 feet into a mist-enshrouded pool.
• Fill your senses with the sights and sounds of a magnificent Douglas-
  fir and western cedar old-growth forest.
• See and hear the roar of cascading water as you view Big Creek
  Gorge from the ridge top.
• Contemplate the perseverance of nature while you view green
  gardens of hanging ferns and mosses clinging to vertical basalt cliffs.
• Be captivated by the spectacular vista view of the upper Lewis River
  as it winds through a forested valley.
• Reach a rocky promontory and scan the rimrock across the way.
  You'll be rewarded with a view of Hemlock Creek free-falling to the
  valley below.

Trail Facts: This maintained trail follows a predominately level
grade. It travels along the ridge top above Big Creek and descends
slightly as you approach a rocky promontory high above the Lewis
River.

Considerations: Extreme caution should be used when approaching
the waterfall. The drop-offs are dangerously steep. The trail ends
abruptly at a rocky promontory high above the Lewis River.

Connections:

• No direct connections. Big Creek Falls is one of many waterfalls along Forest Road 90 accessed by short-distance hikes. Other waterfalls to explore in the area are Lower Lewis Falls, Middle Falls, and Upper Falls (See Lewis River Trail #31). Curly and Miller Creek falls are located nearby, accessed by Forest Road 9039.

Map: Burnt Peak quadrangle.

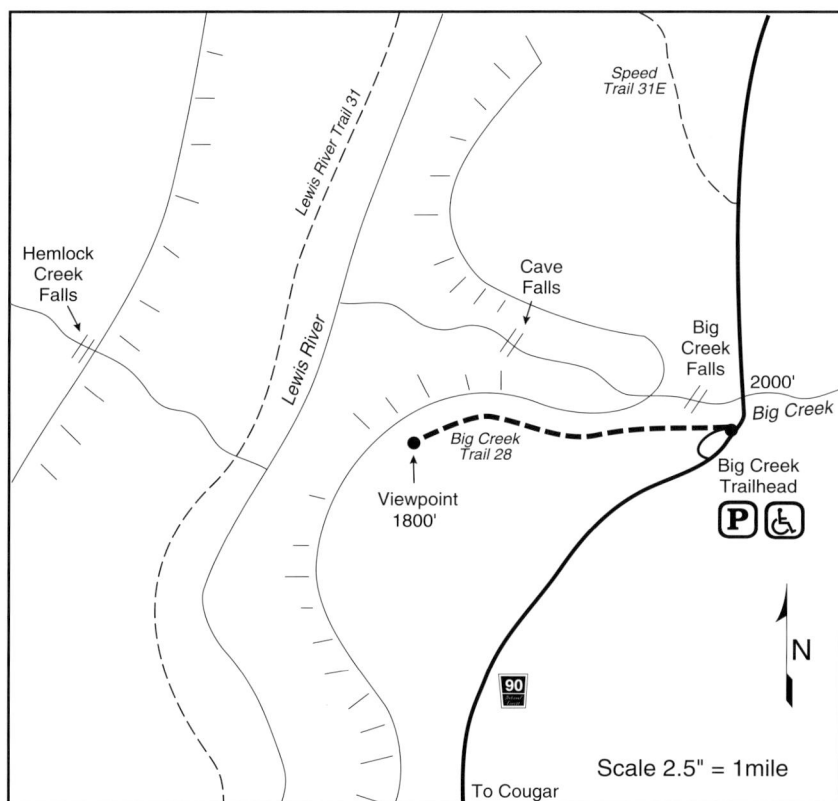

Spencer Butte Trail #30

──────── Users ──────── Difficulty ──────── Facilities ────────

Location: begins, Lower Trailhead Forest Road 93; ends, Upper
Trailhead (end of primitive road near Spencer Meadow).
Length: 1.5 miles to Spencer Butte (one way). 3.0 for trailhead to
trailhead (one way)
Elevation: 3400 feet, low point; 4250 feet, high point
Season: early summer to fall
Use: low

Trail Talk:
• Take a moment to scan Spencer Meadow for elk which are often
found grazing or resting there.
• As you ascend watch for western white pines that have been gouged
or scarred by black bears searching for food beneath the bark.
• As you climb in elevation, watch for changes in the forest. The soft
shapes of pines gradually give way to the tall, slender spires of noble
and subalpine firs.
• At the summit the skyline is dominated by a commanding view of the
volcano. The adventurous can search along the edge of the butte for
the rock arch that perfectly frames Mount St. Helens.
• Discover the remains of an old Forest Service fire lookout built in 1935.
• In the summer months enjoy the colorful tapestry of wildflowers on
the top of Spencer Butte.
• Descend to the Lower Trailhead (Forest Road 93) through a Douglas-
fir forest.

Trail Facts: Spencer Butte is accessed by two different trailheads.
The lower end of the trail climbs through a Douglas-fir forest. The
upper end starts near Spencer Meadow at the end of a primitive road.
This route provides open views through a forest of western white pine.
The entire route is maintained and ascends steadily from each trailhead
to the summit of the butte.

Considerations: No water is available and the trail ascends at a fairly steep grade (20%).

Connections:
• Near Spencer Meadow, it connects with Wildcat Trail #25.
• Breezy Point trail #30A is a side trail to an old fire lookout site. This trail is under construction and is not complete to Breezy Point at present.

Map: Spencer Butte quadrangle.

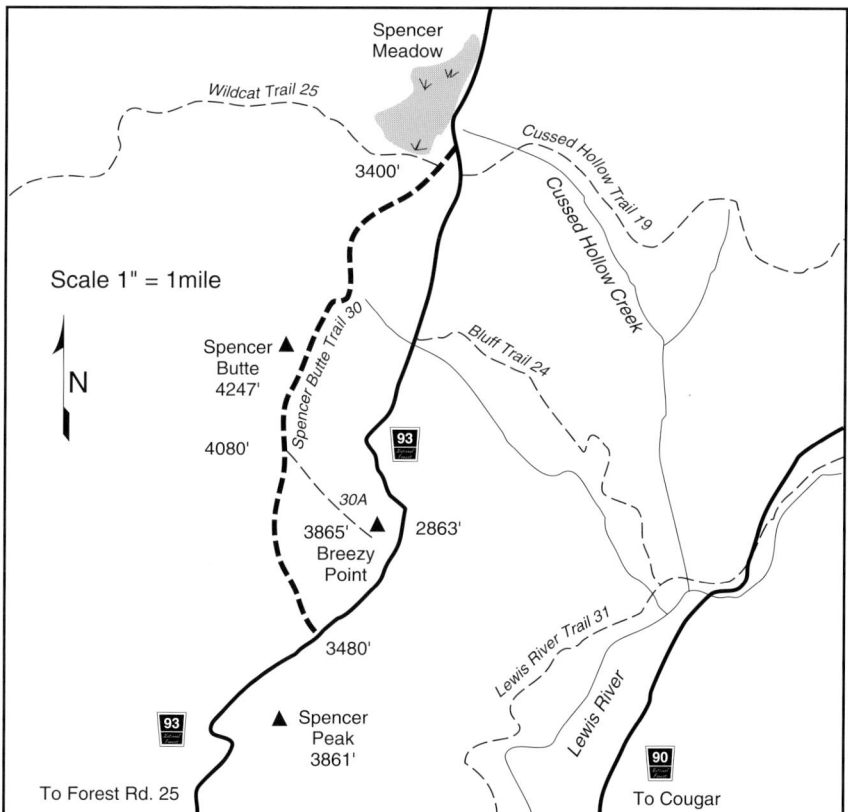

Lewis River Trail #31

This lowland trail follows the course of the Lewis River as it meanders through a magnificent old-growth forest of Douglas-fir, western redcedar and bigleaf maple. Five spectacular waterfalls will delight you as you explore this route. The trail totals 14.4 miles in length, but can be accessed at five different points: Curly Creek viewpoint on Forest Road 9039, the Upper Lewis River bridge on Forest Road 90, Lower Falls Recreation Area on Forest Road 9054, Middle Falls Trailhead on Forest Road 90 and Quartz Creek Trailhead on Forest Road 90. The trail description is broken into three sections. The first section is the barrier-free portion that takes you to views of Curly Creek and Miller Creek falls. The second section starts at Curly Creek viewpoint, heads north and ends at Lower Falls Recreation Area. The third section describes the trail from Lower Falls Recreation Area to the trail's end at its junction with Quartz Creek Trail #5. Come and discover the beauty of the Valley of the Falls.

Map: Burnt Peak, Spencer Butte, and Quartz Creek Butte quadrangle.

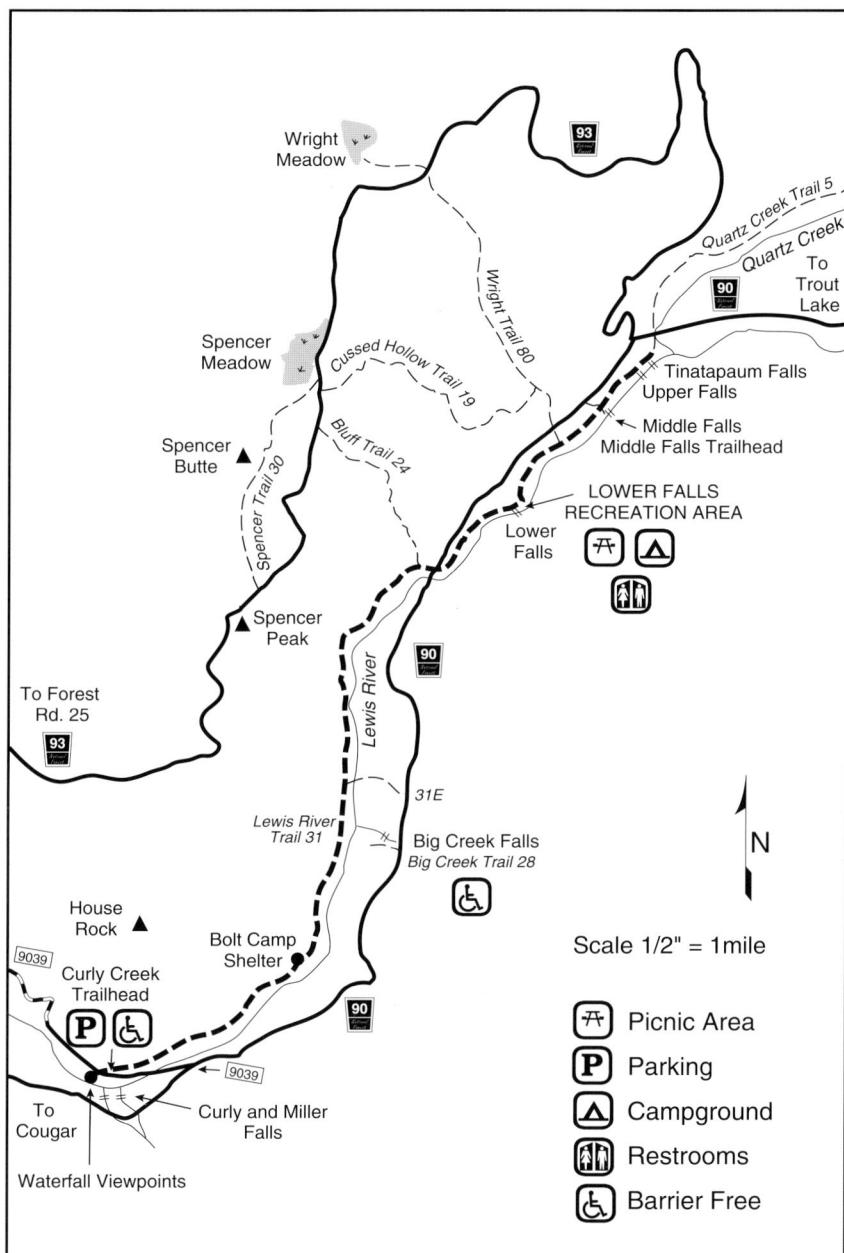

Wright Meadow

93

Quartz Creek Trail 5

Quartz Creek

To Trout Lake

90

Spencer Meadow

Cussed Hollow Trail 19

Wright Trail 80

Tinatapaum Falls
Upper Falls

Middle Falls
Middle Falls Trailhead

Spencer Trail 30

Bluff Trail 24

Spencer Butte

LOWER FALLS
RECREATION AREA

Lower Falls

Spencer Peak

Lewis River

90

To Forest Rd. 25

93

31E

Lewis River Trail 31

Big Creek Falls
Big Creek Trail 28

N

House Rock

9039

Curly Creek Trailhead

Bolt Camp Shelter

P

Scale 1/2" = 1mile

9039

90

To Cougar

Curly and Miller Falls

Waterfall Viewpoints

Picnic Area

P Parking

Campground

Restrooms

Barrier Free

Curly and Miller Creek Falls
Trail #31

——— Users ——— Difficulty ——— Facilities ———

Location: begins, Lewis River Trailhead, Forest Road 9039; ends, Miller Creek Falls Viewpoint
Length: 1/8 mile (one way)
Elevation: 1200 feet
Season: year-round
Use: medium

Trail Talk:
• Enjoy an excellent barrier-free trail that provides a chance for every-one to experience a beautiful setting.
• Peer through the dense evergreen forest and catch a glimpse of the jade green Lewis River flowing through a basalt channel 50 feet below.
• Marvel at nature's handiwork as you contemplate Curly Creek cascading beneath two graceful lava rock arches.
• Walk a little further, and discover Miller Creek plunging over a moss- and fern-laden cliff into the Lewis River below.

Trail Facts: This maintained trail leaves the parking area near the restroom facilities and then traverses along a ridge. The trail's surface is compacted gravel and is 4 feet wide to Curly Creek Falls viewpoint. The trail narrows to 3 feet beyond Curly Creek to its end at Miller Creek Falls.

Considerations: None

Connections:
• The Curly and Miller Creek Falls Trail connects with Lewis River Trail #31.

Map: Spencer Butte and Quartz Creek Butte quadrangles.

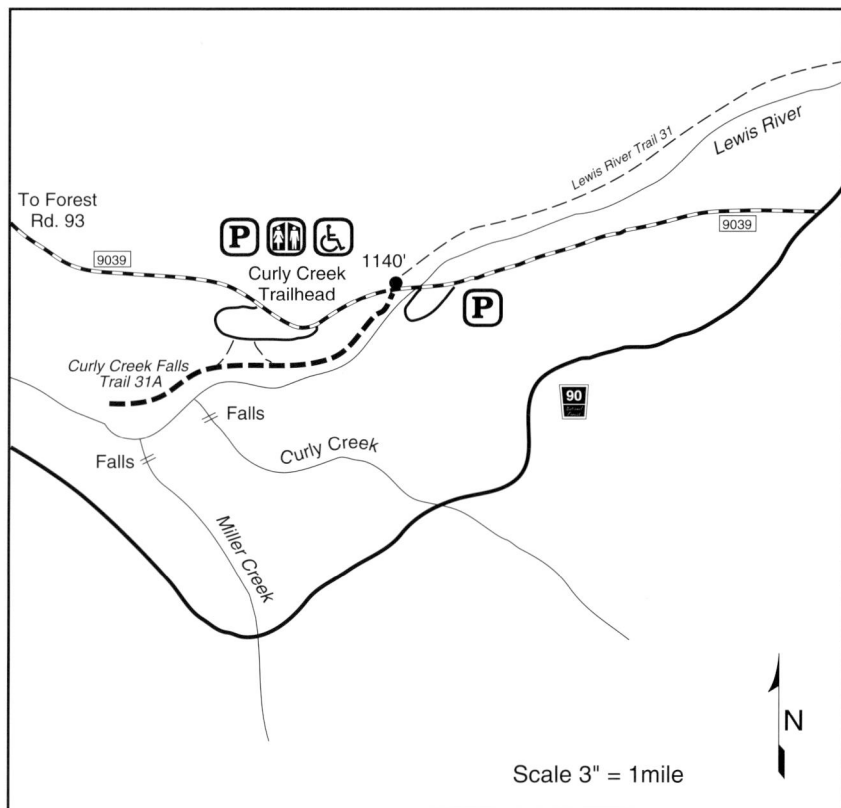

To Forest
Rd. 93

9039

P | ♂♀ | ♿

Curly Creek
Trailhead

1140'

P

Lewis River Trail 31

Lewis River

9039

Curly Creek Falls
Trail 31A

Falls

Falls

Curly Creek

90

Miller Creek

N

Scale 3" = 1mile

Lewis River Trail #31

Curly Creek Trailhead to Lower Falls
Recreation Area segment

———— Users ————   Difficulty   ———— Facilities ————

Location: begins, Curly Creek Trailhead, Forest Road 9039; junctions Lower Falls Recreation Area, Forest Road 9054
Length: 11 miles (one way)
Elevation: 1260 feet, low point; 1800 feet, high point
Season: early spring to fall
Use: medium

Trail Talk:
• Get out and enjoy an early or late season hike while other trails are still beneath the cover of snow.
• Discover picturesque Curly and Miller Creek falls. (See Curly Creek Trail #31).
• Gain access to the wild and scenic Lewis River for fishing, kayaking or rafting opportunities.
• Stroll through an example of a magnificent Douglas-fir, western red cedar and big leaf maple old-growth forest.
• Stop at historic Bolt Camp Shelter (built by the Forest Service in 1921). It was used when they were harvesting cedar bolts for settlements downstream. The shelter was restored in 1991.
• Become saturated with the sights and sounds of water as you hike through this valley laced with abundant side streams, springs, and misty waterfalls.
• Obtain views of the Cascade Gorge carved through basalt cliffs by the relentless Lewis River.
• Linger at the spectacular Lower Lewis River Falls while you watch the river tumble and roar over a terraced cliff.

Trail Facts: This maintained trail remains within sight or sound of the Lewis River. It follows a predominantly level grade until climbing above the Cascade Gorge. The trail then continues across Forest Road 90 and climbs to a breathtaking view of the Lower Lewis River Falls.

Considerations: Water is plentiful along the trail but needs to be treated for safe drinking. Rocks along the shoreline can be extremely slippery and dangerous. During spring runoff, side streams become swollen, making ford crossings more of a challenge.

Connections:
• The Lewis River Trail continues on to a junction with Quartz Creek Trail #5 (see Lower Falls Recreation Area to Quartz Creek Trail #5 segment) .
• Bluff Trail #19 connects with the Lewis River Trail near Cussed Hollow Creek.

Map: Burnt Peak, Spencer Butte, and Quartz Creek Butte quadrangles.

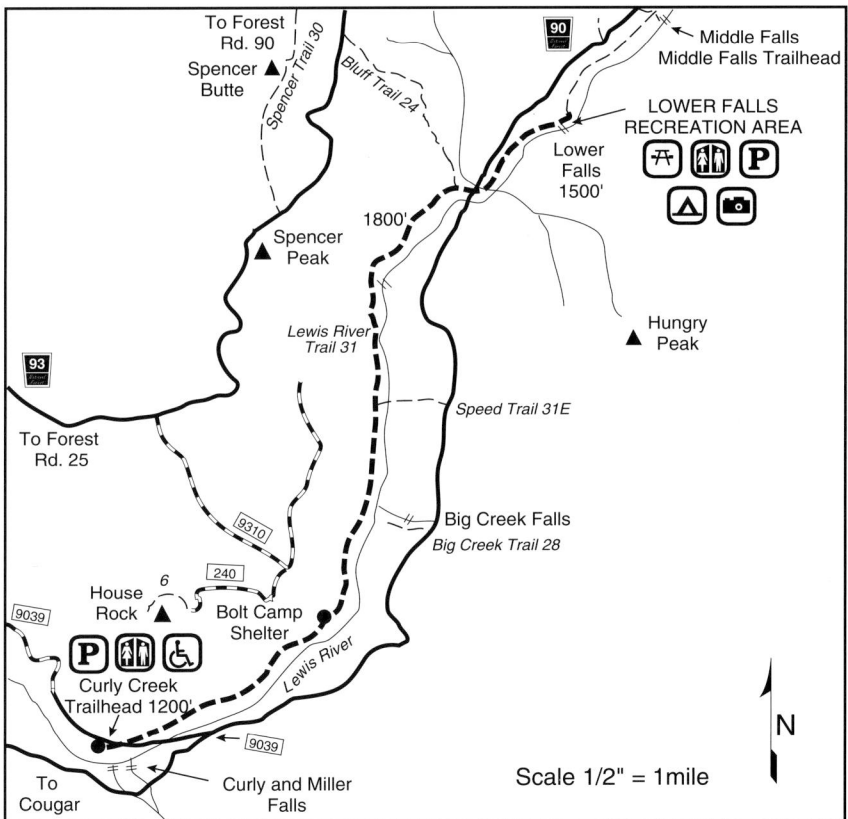

Lewis River Trail #31

Lower Falls Recreation Area to Quartz Creek Trail #5

——— Users ———   Difficulty   ——— Facilities ———

Location: begins, Lower Falls Recreation Area; ends, Quartz Creek Trailhead #5, Forest Road 90

Length: 3.25 miles (one way)

Elevation: 1600 feet, low point; 1800 feet, high point

Season: late spring to fall

Use: medium

Trail Talk:
- Travel through a magnificent Douglas-fir forest to Middle Falls.
- Discover the remains of an old "sheep" bridge and "steam donkey." The steam donkey is believed to have been used to move the bridge in and out of place to avoid winter floods on the river. Sheep from the Trout Lake area were herded across the bridge to gain access to grazing areas on the Randle Ranger District.
- Enjoy the laughing, rushing waters of the Lewis River as they churn and slide over Middle Falls.
- Experience yet another spectacular waterfall as Upper Falls cascades over a horseshoe-shaped cliff.
- The trail ends on the Forest Road 90 near the crystal waters of Quartz Creek.

Trail Facts: This maintained trail leaves the Lower Falls Campground and climbs above the river. It crosses Copper Creek and comes to Middle Falls. The trail circles a cliff above Upper Falls, providing excellent views of the falls. It crosses Alec Creek and terminates on Forest Road 90 near Quartz Creek Trail #5.

Considerations: Rocks at the water's edge can be extremely slippery. Steep cliffs along trail may be dangerous–use caution.

Connections:
• This segment of Lewis River Trail #31 connects with the lower portion of Trail #31 to the south.
• At the northern end it connects with Quartz Creek Trail #5.
• Wright Meadow Trail #80 joins the trail just south of Middle Falls.
• Middle Falls Trail #31C provides access from Middle Falls Trailhead on Forest Road 90 to Lewis River Trail #31.

Map: Spencer Butte and Quartz Creek Butte quadrangles.

Middle Falls Trail #31C

———— Users ———— Difficulty ——— Facilities ————

Location: begins, Middle Falls Trailhead Forest Road 90; ends, Middle Falls
Length: 3/4 mile (loop)
Elevation: 1760 feet, high point; 1520 feet, low point
Season: spring to fall
Use: medium

Trail Talk:
• Hike into a lush and deep green Douglas-fir forest.
• Cross over a rustic bridge that spans Copper Creek.
• Discover the misty veil of Copper Creek cascading down a 40-foot basalt cliff.
• Descend to the Lewis River and discover the churning chute of Middle Falls.

Trail Facts: This maintained trail is relatively level until passing Copper Creek Falls. Beyond there the descent steepens to the Middle Falls of the Lewis River. A loop opportunity is available by crossing Copper Creek on the lower bridge and then taking the trail junction to the right.

Considerations: Rocks along the water's edge can be extremely slippery.

Connections:
• Middle Falls Trail #31C connects with Lewis River Trail #31.

Map: Spencer Butte and Quartz Creek Butte quadrangle.

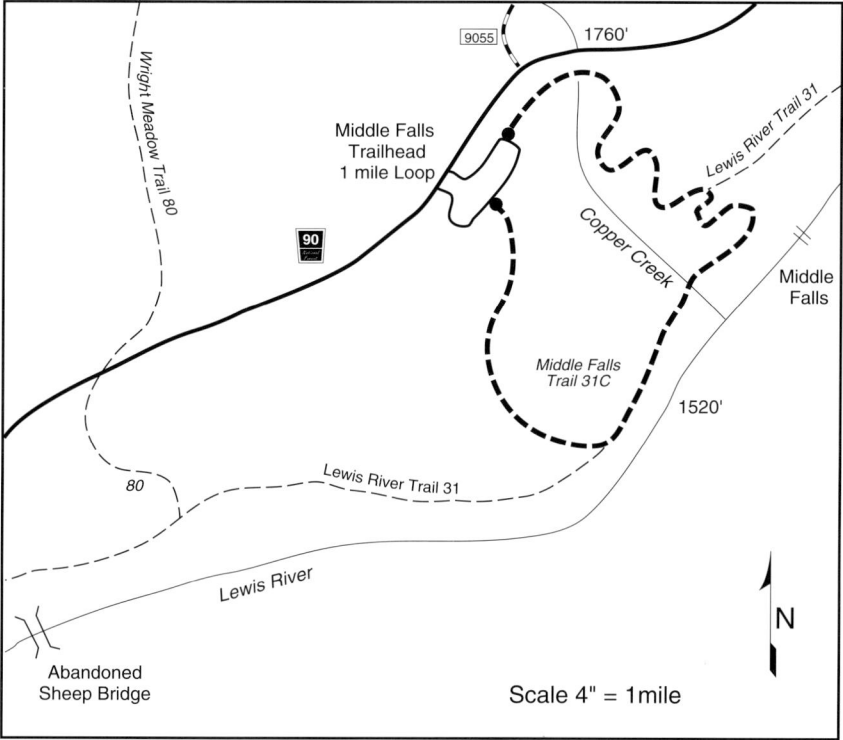

Wright Meadow Trail 80

9055   1760'

Middle Falls
Trailhead
1 mile Loop

Lewis River Trail 31

90

Copper Creek

Middle
Falls

Middle Falls
Trail 31C

1520'

80   Lewis River Trail 31

Lewis River

N

Abandoned
Sheep Bridge

Scale 4" = 1mile

Speed Trail #31E

───────── Users ─────────   Difficulty   ───────── Facilities ─────────

Location: begins, Forest Road 90; ends, Lewis River
Length: 1 mile (one way)
Elevation: 1800 feet, high point; 1200 feet, low point
Season: spring to fall
Use: low

Trail Talk:
• Hike through a stand of old-growth forest near the drainage of Big
  Creek.
• Access the middle section of the Lewis River for remote fishing
  opportunities.
• Ford the river to connect with the scenic Lewis River Trail.

Trail Facts: This maintained trail is a steep descent through old-
growth timber. It provides quick fishing access to the Lewis River and
connects with the Lewis River Trail #31 via a ford crossing.

Considerations: The trail is extremely steep in some sections.
Fording the Lewis River is possible only during the summer months
(after mid-July) due to heavy spring runoff.

Connections:
• Speed Trail #31E connects with Lewis River Trail #31 via river
  crossing.

Map: Burnt Peak quadrangle.

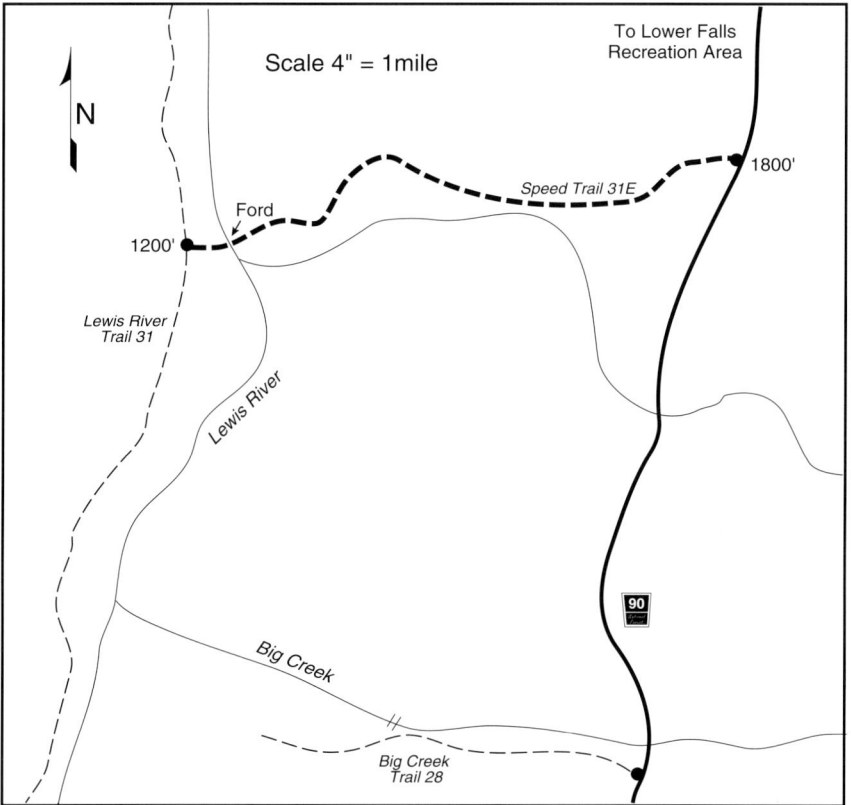

Wright Meadow Trail #80

——— Users ———   Difficulty   ——— Facilities ———

Location: begins, Lewis River Trail or Forest Road 90; ends, Forest Road 2559-100 to 101
Length: 7.5 miles (one way)
Elevation: 1756 feet, low point; 3200 feet, high point
Season: late spring to fall
Use: low

Trail Talk:
• Climb through a mature forest to the intersection of Cussed Hollow Trail #19.
• Cross a fork of Copper Creek via a newly constructed bridge and enter into a managed forest with clearcut openings.
• Relax at the campsite on Wright Creek located at 9327/040 Forest Road junction.
• Discover Wright Meadow, a grassy glade surrounded by forest.
• Watch for elk grazing in the meadow.
• Explore the area near the confluence of Elk and Clear creeks and discover the impressive Clear Creek gorge.

Trail Facts: This maintained trail passes through a diverse forest setting. It ascends from the Lewis River Trail, crosses Road 90 and continues on through the forest to Road 9328. After passing through clearcuts and along a road segment, you reenter the forest in the Clear Creek Roadless Area. The trail ends in a clearcut just below Forest Road 2559-101 spur. Possible campsites are near the new bridge across the fork of Copper Creek and in the trees near Wright Meadow.

Considerations: This trail offers an excellent opportunity for horseback riding from the Lewis River Trail #31 to Craggy Peak Trail #2. A ford of Clear Creek is necessary.

Connections:

• Wright Meadow Trail #80 connects with Lewis River Trail #31, and Cussed Hollow Trail #19.
• It also connects with Craggy Peak Trail #3.

Map: Spencer Butte and Quartz Creek Butte quadrangles.

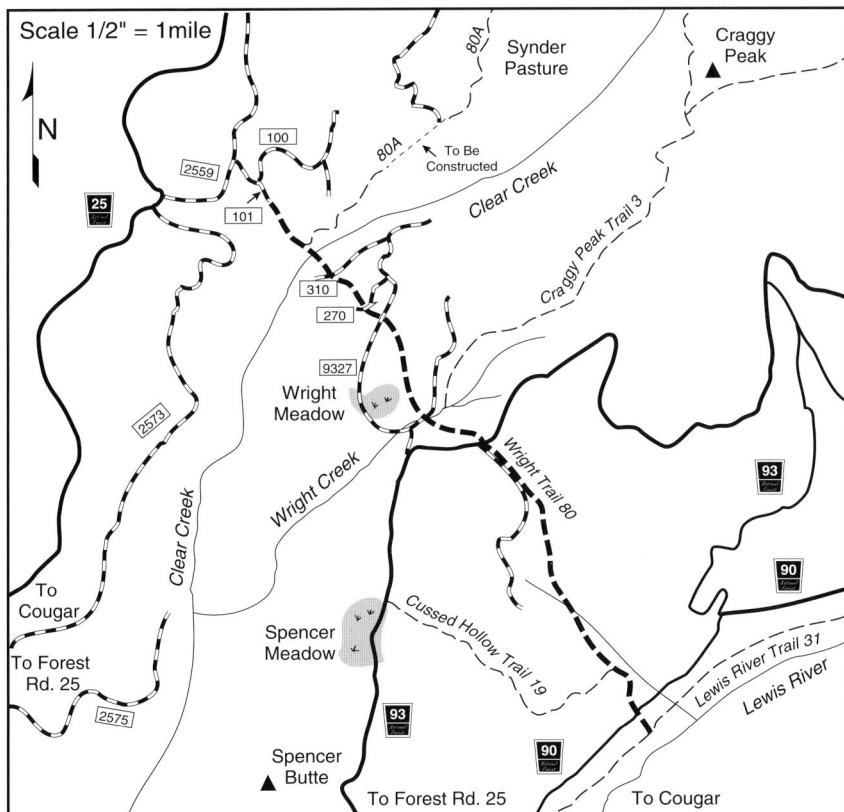

Lava Canyon Trail #184

—— Users —— Difficulty —— Facilities ——

Location: begins, Lava Canyon Trailhead, Forest Road 83; ends, Smith Creek Trail #225

Length: upper section– 0.5 miles (one way)

middle section– 0.5 mile (one way)

lower section– 2.0 miles (one way)

Elevation: 3000 feet, high point; 1570 feet, low point
Season: summer to fall
Use: upper section: high; lower and middle section: low

Trail Talk:

• Lava Canyon is a dynamic art gallery where the natural world displays its powerful works. Mount St. Helens, water, and the forest are sculpting and painting the canyon. As the Muddy River plummets 1,400 feet down the canyon, powerful waterfalls cascade over ancient rock. If you wish to follow the river's journey, be prepared to travel as it does:

Upper section:
• Stroll along this paved and boardwalk trail.
• Relax and reflect upon the spectacular beauty and design of nature.

Middle section:
• Venture along this loop trail and cross over the turbulent Muddy River.
• Walk in the shadow of a lava flow.

Lower Section:
• Descend into the depths of the canyon as you follow the Muddy River as it carves its way down a rugged landscape.

Considerations: Beware of slick rocks and steep drops. For your safety, please stay on the trail. The masterpieces in the gallery are fragile and irreplaceable. Please respect the natural features. This trail is closed to mountain bike, trail bike, and pack and saddle users. Although the first section of trail is barrier free, be aware that it is a more difficult barrier-free trail with grades approaching 12%.

Connections:
• Trail #184 connects with Smith Creek Trail #225 at its lower end.

Map: Smith Creek Butte quadrangle.

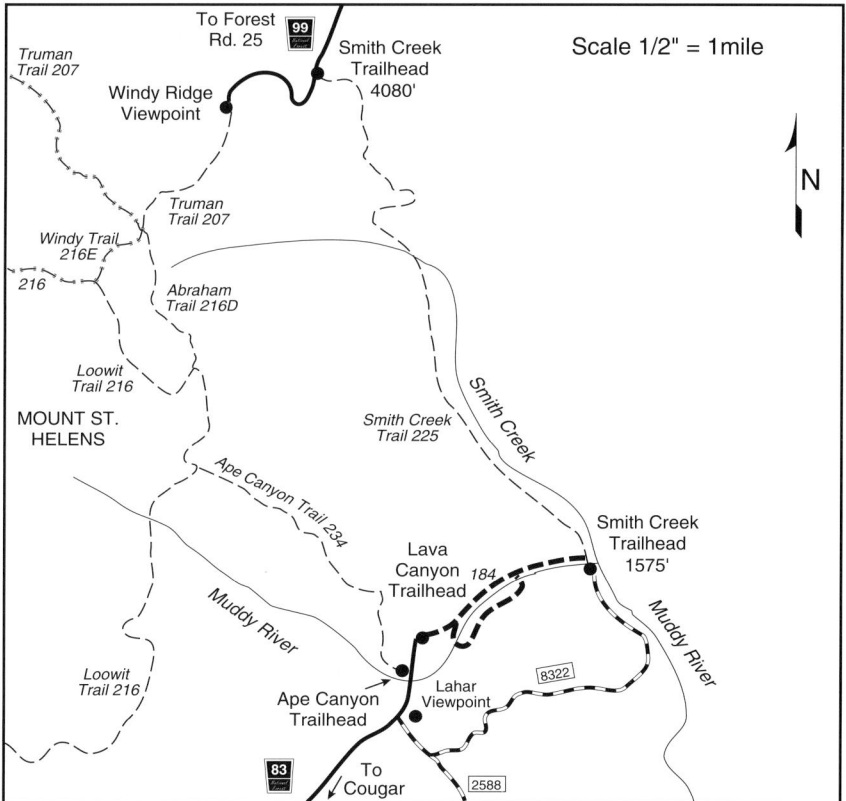

Goat Creek Trail #205

———— Users ————   Difficulty   ———— Facilities ————

Location: begins, Road 2750; ends, Goat Mt. Trail #217
Length: 5.5 miles (one way)
Elevation: 4680 feet, high point; 2400 feet, low point
Season: May–October
Use: upper section: high; lower and middle section: low

Trail Talk:
• Discover views and sounds of the wild water of Goat Creek and its
  many tributaries.
• Hike through an undisturbed forest of Douglas-fir and western red
  cedar, where wind knocks the mighty trees over, exposing large root
  systems.
• Listen quietly for the sounds of wildlife and search for sign of deer
  and elk.
• Enjoy vistas of the Goat Creek Basin.

Trail Facts: Trail quickly joins Goat Creek after an unforgettable
waterfall experience. The trail follows Goat Creek upstream to junction
with Tumwater Trail #218. The trail then turns west and ascends the
west fork Goat Creek drainages, crossing tributaries with waterfalls.
The trail crosses the creek twice in its ascent. Switchback up through
forest with opening of views to the forested drainage below. The trail
passes next to open meadows and rock cliffs as it joins Goat Mtn. Trail
#217 just south of Vanson Peak.

Considerations: Treat water before drinking. Winter storms may
affect trail conditions. For early season hiking on this trail please call
Monument Headquarters (206) 247-5473 for current trail condition.

Connections:
• Goat Creek Trail #205 connects to Goat Mtn. Trail #217 and Tumwater Trail #218.

Map: Vanson Peak and Cowlitz Falls quadrangles.

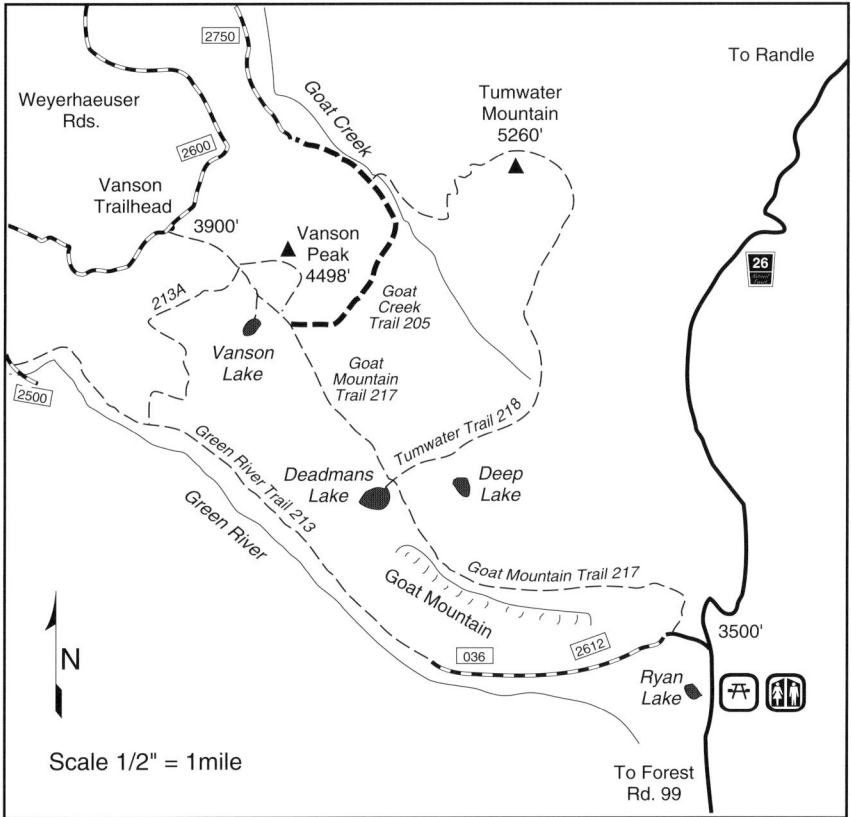

Truman Trail #207

———— Users ———— Difficulty ——— Facilities ————

Location: begins, Windy Ridge Trailhead Forest Road 99; ends, Boundary Trail #1
Length: 6.5 miles (one way)
Elevation: 3600 feet, low point; 4200 feet, high point
Season: summer to fall
Use: medium

Trail Talk:
• Hike on newly created terrain. The Truman Trail traverses the pyroclastic flow and debris avalanche deposits north of the crater of Mount St. Helens.
• Discover the new plant life returning to the area and learn about the research that scientists are conducting to follow this dynamic process.
• Walk in awe of the magnitude of the effects which the eruption had upon this landscape.
• Enjoy breathtaking views of the steaming dome and the still waters of Spirit Lake.

Trail Facts: This maintained trail begins at the Windy Ridge Trailhead on Forest Road 99. It descends in elevation, following an old road bed. The trail then traverses the pumice plain and it is located by wooden post route markers. It then ascends in elevation to its junction with Boundary Trail #1.

Considerations: This is an extremely fragile environment; please note all restrictions in the area. This trail closed to mountain bikes. No water is available along the trail and shade from the sun is nonexistent. Allow 3-1/2 to 4 hours round trip from Windy Ridge to reach views of the lava dome.

Restricted Area: Travel allowed on approved trails only. Off-trail travel and camping are prohibited to protect sensitive natural features and scientific studies. Research permits are required for off-trail travel.

Connections:
• The trail connects to Abraham Trail #216D.
• Windy Trail #216E forms the connection between the Truman Trail #207 and the Loowit Trail #216.
• The Truman Trail terminates at its junction with Boundary Trail #1.

Map: Mount St. Helens, Spirit Lake West quadrangles.

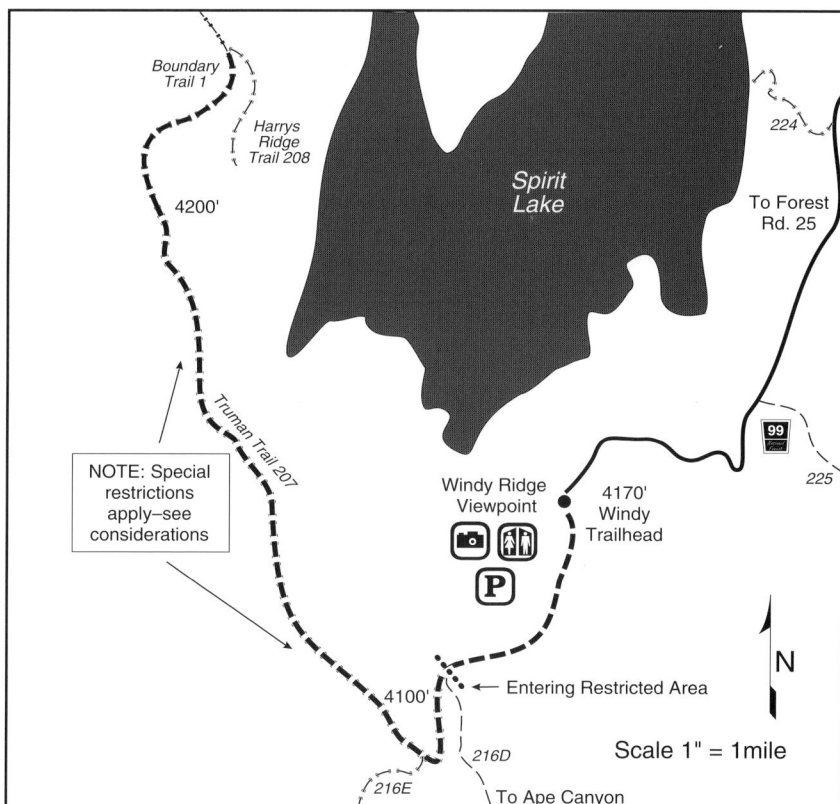

Harrys Ridge Trail #208

──── Users ──── Difficulty ──── Facilities ────

Location: begins, Boundary Trail #1; ends, Harrys Ridge Viewpoint
Length: .6 miles (one way)
Elevation: 4400 feet, lower point; 4600 feet, higher point
Season: summer to fall
Use: low

Trail Talk:
• Obtain one of the best and most direct views into the crater of Mount St. Helens.
• Gaze across Spirit Lake's west arm and south shore.
• Discover Harrys Ridge where the debris avalanche scoured the surface to bedrock.

Trail Facts: This maintained trail follows a predominantly level grade along Harrys Ridge. Its only access is from Boundary Trail #1.

Considerations: No water is available along this trail.

Restricted Area: Travel allowed on approved trails only. Off-trail travel and camping are prohibited to protect sensitive natural features and scientific studies. Research permits are required for off-trail travel.

Connections:
• Harrys Ridge Trail is accessed by the Boundary Trail #1 and Truman Trail #207.

Map: Spirit Lake West quadrangle.

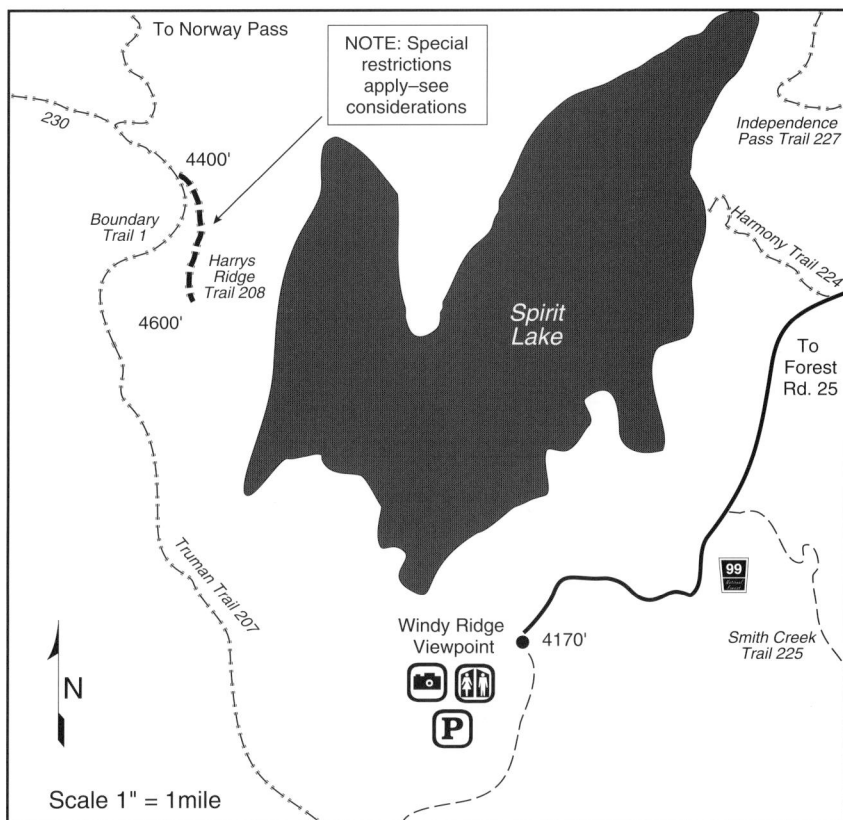

To Norway Pass

NOTE: Special
restrictions
apply—see
considerations

230

4400'

Boundary
Trail 1

Harrys
Ridge
Trail 208

4600'

Truman Trail 207

*Spirit
Lake*

Independence
Pass Trail 227

Harmony Trail 224

To
Forest
Rd. 25

99

Smith Creek
Trail 225

Windy Ridge
Viewpoint

4170'

N

Scale 1" = 1mile

Meta Lake Trail #210

———— Users ————   Difficulty   ———— Facilities ————

Location: begins, Meta Lake Trailhead, or Miner's Car, Forest Road
    99; ends, Meta Lake
Length: .25 mile (one way)
Elevation: 3610 feet
Season: early summer to fall
Use: high

Trail Talk:
• Enjoy an easy stroll along a paved path that provides barrier-free
  access into the blast zone.
• Marvel at how life survived only 8 1/2 miles from the volcano
  because it was hidden beneath a sheltering blanket of snow and ice.
• Imagine the small surviving trees around you becoming the towering
  forest of tomorrow.
• Meta Lake's shores and waters teem with aquatic life (eastern brook
  trout, salamanders and frogs).
• Discover the swarms of squirming tadpoles that crowd the lakeshore
  each summer. (July is best.)

Trail Facts: This maintained trail follows a level grade to Meta Lake.
The paved surface is 3 1/2 feet wide. The trail returns via the same
route.

Considerations: Meta Lake offers barrier-free access into the blast
zone. Stay on the trail and lakeshore viewing platform to ensure that
others may enjoy the recovering vegetation.

Connections:
• Meta Lake is one of many trails along Forest Road 99 offering you
the opportunity to explore the Mount St. Helens National Volcanic
Monument. Independence Pass Trail #227, Boundary Trail #1, Har-

mony Trail #224, and Windy Ridge Sand Ladder #242 are all short-distance hikes, but they vary in their degrees of difficulty.

Map: Spirit Lake East quadrangle.

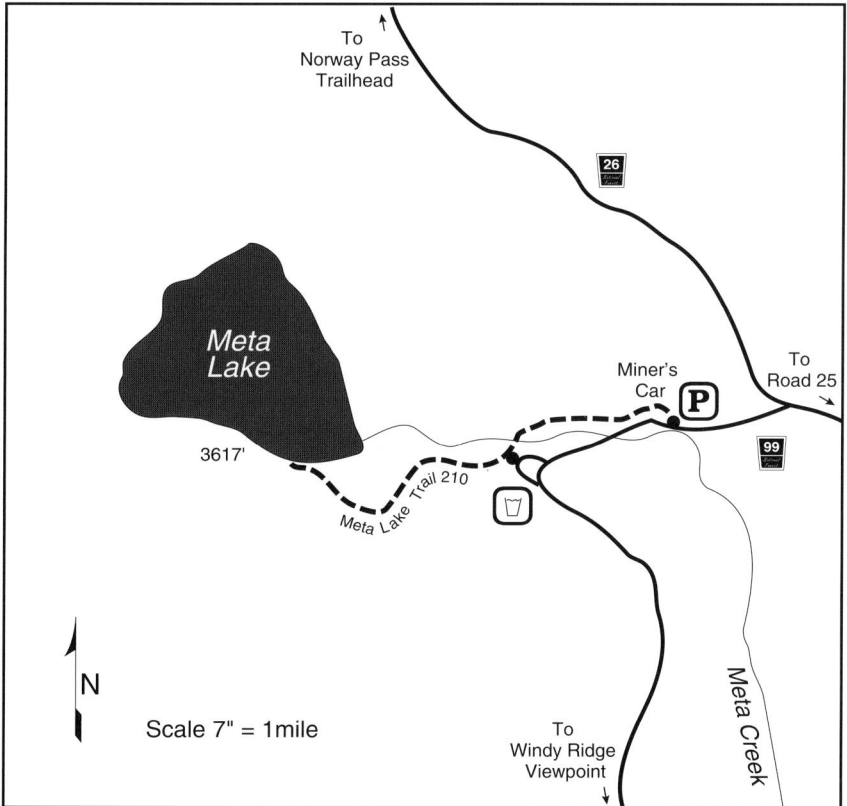

Lakes Trail #211
and Elk Bench Trail #211D

——— Users ——— Difficulty ——— Facilities ———

Location: begins, Coldwater Lake Boat Launch or Elk Bench Trail-head at Coldwater Ridge Visitor Center; ends, junction with Coldwater Trail #230

Length: 5.25 miles (one way); Elk Bench Trail 0.5 mile (one way)

Elevation: 3120 feet, high point; 2500 feet, low point

Season: April–November

Use: high

Trail Talk:
- Enjoy sparkling view of Coldwater Lake, Minnie Peak and Mount St. Helens.
- Discover the lake formed by the volcanic dam of the debris avalanche.
- Be amazed by the amount of returning plant life–cottonwood beaches, birds, deer, and elk can all be viewed along this trail.
- Watch for the phosphorescent rainbow trout coming to the surface to eat.
- A brand new shoreline is being formed as wind, rain and ice break down the sides of the lake and deposit the new material creating a shallow shelf and new shoreline.

Trail Facts: From Elk Bench Trailhead, Elk Bench Trail #210 descends to junction with Lakes Trail #211. The Lakes Trail skirts the edge of Coldwater Lake from the boat launch to Coldwater Creek at the NE end of the lake. Along the way the trail crosses wet marsh areas and follows Coldwater Creek to the junction with Coldwater Trail #230.

Considerations: Treat water before drinking.

Connections:
- Lakes Trail #211 connects with Coldwater Trail #230 which connects to Boundary Trail #1. This offers a cross-monument hiking experience.

Map: Elk Rock and Spirit Lake West quadrangles.

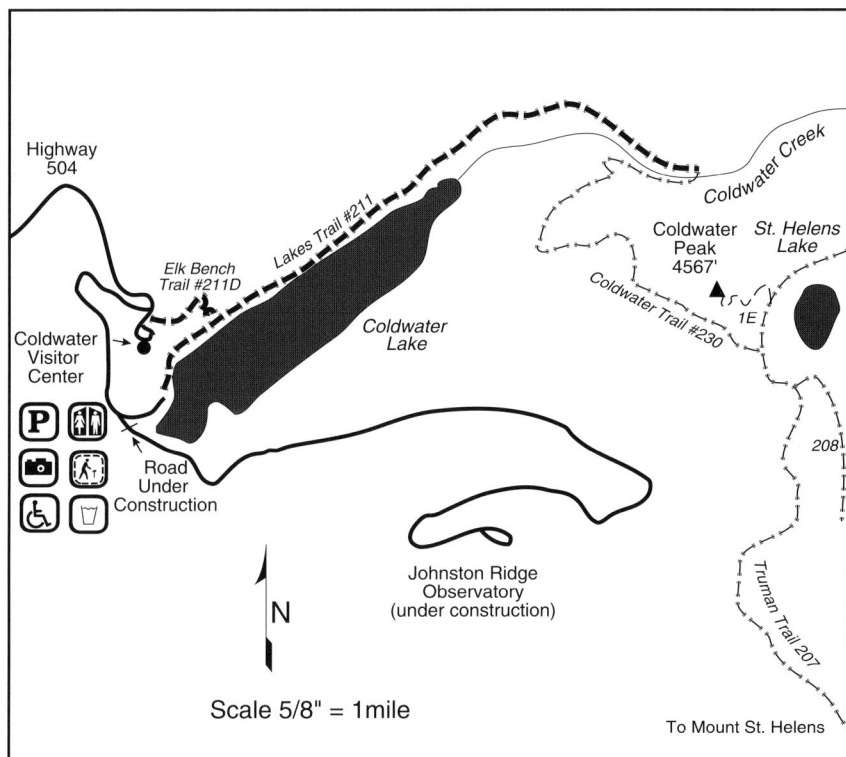

Green River Trail #213

Users ———— Difficulty ———— Facilities

Location: begins, Forest Road 2612; ends, Weyerhaeuser Road 2500.
Length: 7.5 miles (one way)
Elevation: 2560 feet, high point; 1880 feet, low point
Season: summer to fall
Use: low

Trail Talk:
• Hike a historic route that was blazed as early as 1897 to access
  mining claims along the Green River.
• Contrast the tranquility and solitude the trail now offers with the
  bustling mining activity of the bygone era.
• Be respectful of any remnants of the area's cultural history by leaving
  them undisturbed.
• Marvel at the magnificence of an old-growth forest.
• Listen to the melodic sounds of the Green River as you meander
  close beside it.

Trail Facts: This maintained trail travels along the Green River
through an old-growth forest.

Considerations: Water should be treated for safe drinking. Preserve
the special beauty of this old-growth forest by using no-trace camping
and user methods. The Archeological Resources Protection Act of
1979 makes removal of artifacts from federal lands illegal.

Connections:
• The Green River Trail #213 connects with Vanson Ridge Trail
  #213A, which provides access to Goat Mountain Trail #217.

Map: Spirit Lake East, Cowlitz Falls, and Vanson Peak quadrangles.

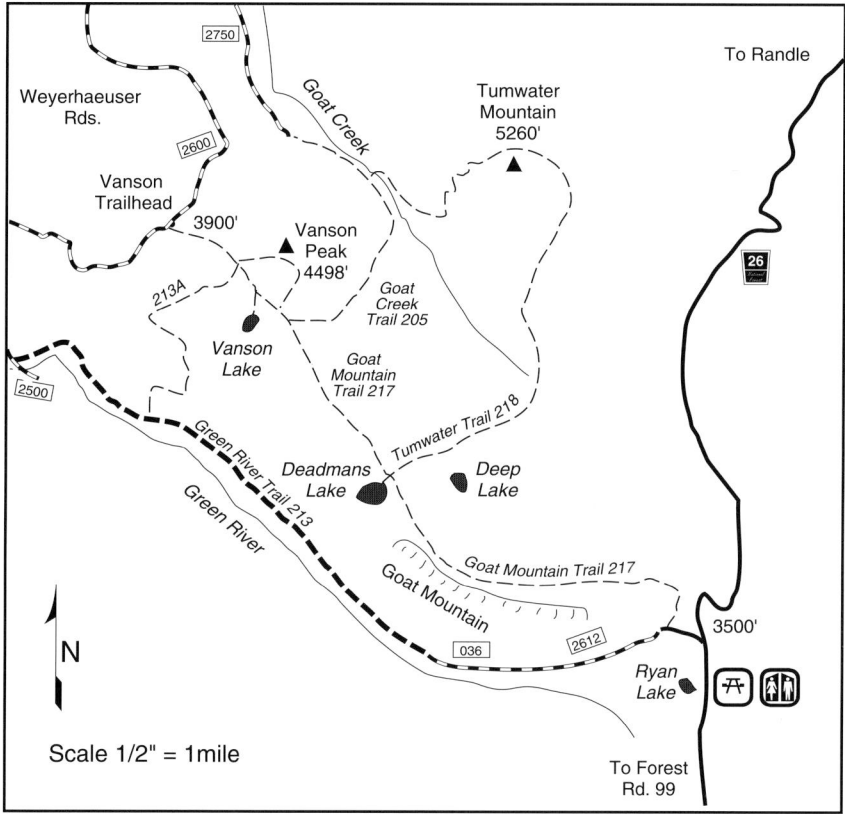

2750

To Randle

Weyerhaeuser
Rds.

2600

Goat Creek

Tumwater
Mountain
5260'

Vanson
Trailhead

3900'

Vanson
Peak
4498'

213A

26

Goat
Creek
Trail 205

Vanson
Lake

Goat
Mountain
Trail 217

2500

Tumwater Trail 218

Green River Trail 213

Deadmans
Lake

Deep
Lake

Green River

Goat Mountain Trail 217

Goat Mountain

036

2612

3500'

N

Ryan
Lake

Scale 1/2" = 1mile

To Forest
Rd. 99

Vanson Ridge Trail #213A

——— Users ———   Difficulty   ——— Facilities ———

Location: begins, Goat Mountain Trail #217; ends, Green River Trail #213

Length: 3.3 miles (one way)

Elevation: 4200 feet, high point; 2200 feet, low point

Season: summer to fall

Use: low

Trail Talk:
- Hike through a dense evergreen forest of Douglas-fir and Pacific silver fir.
- Enjoy views of the Green River and Falls Creek drainages.
- Cross numerous small rivulets.
- Enjoy an extensive excursion that takes you from the serenity of an old-growth forest to expansive views of the Cascade Range by hiking a loop that incorporates Goat Mountain Trail #217, Vanson Ridge Trail #213A and Green River Trail #213.

Trail Facts: This maintained trail descends at a 20 to 30 percent grade to connect the Goat Mountain Trail #216 to Green River Trail #213.

Considerations: Because of steep grades, it is best to hike down Vanson Ridge Trail #213A from Goat Mountain Trail #217. Water is available but should be treated for safe drinking.

Connections:
- Trail #213A forms the connection between Goat Mountain Trail #217 and Green River Trail #213.

Map: Vanson Peak quadrangle.

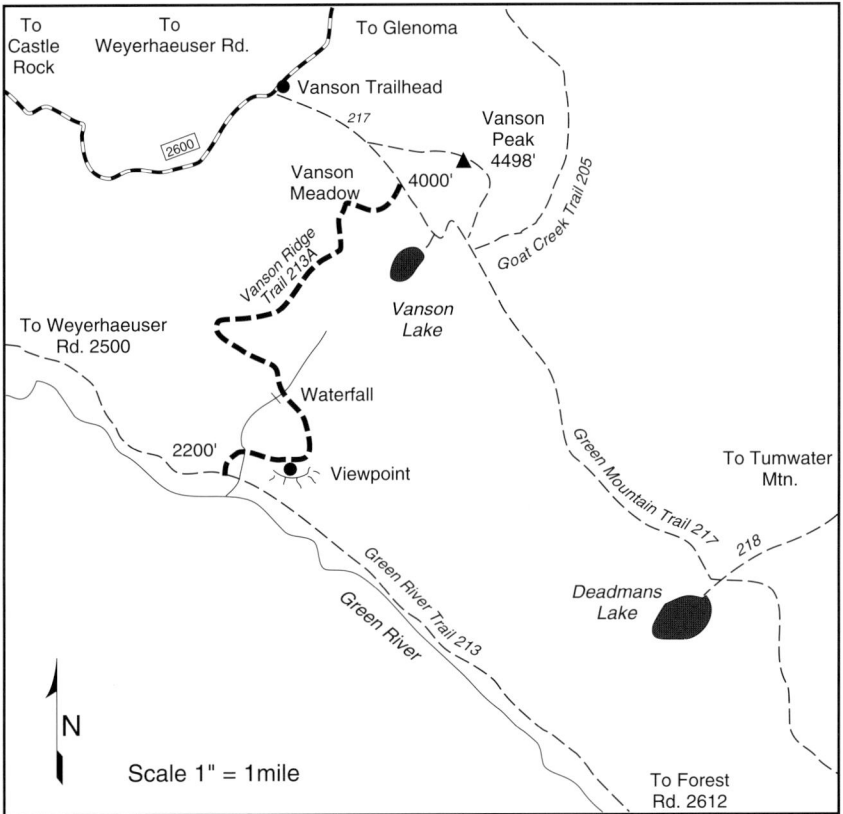

To Castle Rock

To Weyerhaeuser Rd.

To Glenoma

Vanson Trailhead

2600

217

Vanson Peak 4498'

Vanson Meadow

4000'

Goat Creek Trail 205

Vanson Ridge Trail 213A

To Weyerhaeuser Rd. 2500

Vanson Lake

Waterfall

2200'

Viewpoint

Green Mountain Trail 217

To Tumwater Mtn.

218

Green River Trail 213

Green River

Deadmans Lake

N

Scale 1" = 1mile

To Forest Rd. 2612

Ptarmigan Trail #216A

——— Users ——— Difficulty ——— Facilities ———

Location: begins, climbers' bivouac, Road 8100-830; ends, Monitor Ridge climbing route
Length: 2.1 miles (one way)
Elevation: 3600 feet, low point; 4500 feet, high point
Season: spring to fall
Use: high

Trail Talk:
• Gain direct access to Mount St. Helens' most popular climbing route, Monitor Ridge.
• Enjoy views of Mount St. Helens, Mount Hood, Mount Adams and Yale Reservoir.
• Travel through forest until breaking out onto the open slopes of Mount St. Helens. A massive lava flow looms at the trail's end.

Trail Facts: This maintained trail passes through the forest, terminating at the edge of a large lava flow on the open slopes of Mount St. Helens. It provides direct access to the Monitor Ridge climbing route. A climbers' bivouac is located at the trailhead.

Considerations: For travel above 4800 feet a permit is required. Those climbing Mount St. Helens can obtain more information by requesting a copy of the Climbers' Brochure or contacting Mount St. Helens National Volcanic Monument Headquarters. Water is unavailable at the climbers' bivouac.

Connections:
• Ptarmigan Trail #216A connects directly into the Monitor Ridge climbing route and the Loowit Trail system.

Map: Mount St. Helens quadrangle.

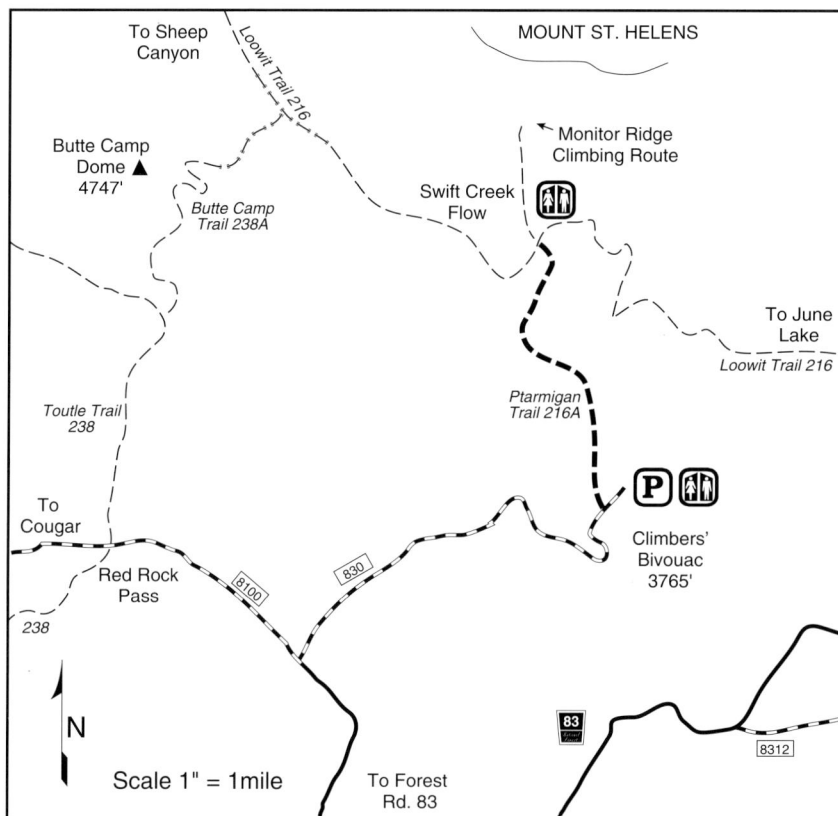

To Sheep Canyon

Loowit Trail 216

MOUNT ST. HELENS

Butte Camp Dome ▲ 4747'

Butte Camp Trail 238A

Monitor Ridge Climbing Route

Swift Creek Flow

To June Lake

Loowit Trail 216

Toutle Trail 238

Ptarmigan Trail 216A

To Cougar

P

Red Rock Pass

8100

830

Climbers' Bivouac 3765'

238

N

83

8312

Scale 1" = 1mile

To Forest Rd. 83

June Lake Trail #216B

——— Users ——— Difficulty ——— Facilities ———

Location: begins, June Lake Trailhead, Forest Road 83; ends, Loowit
  Trail #216
Length: 1.4 miles (one way)
Elevation: 2710 feet, low point; 3400 feet, high point
Season: year-round
Use: medium

Trail Talk:
• Take a gentle climb through a young fir forest as you follow along
  the course of June Creek.
• The ease and short distance make this trail an enjoyable family
  outing.
• Stop and picnic at beautiful and unique June Lake. The lake lies
  nestled along the base of a basalt cliff over which a waterfall pours to
  replenish the lake's cold, clear water.
• On the south shore an inviting sandy beach is bordered by a massive
  lava flow and Mount St. Helens looms just out of sight.
• Discover the crystalline beauty of this setting by cross-country skiing
  during the winter months.

Trail Facts: This maintained trail climbs gently but steadily to June
Lake. From there, it's a steep ascent to the junction with the Loowit
Trail system.

Considerations: Preserve June Lake's unique beauty by practicing
low impact hiking and camping ethics.

Connections:
• June Lake Trail #216B connects directly into the Loowit Trail
  system. During the winter months it becomes a cross-country ski trail.

Map: Mount St. Helens quadrangle.

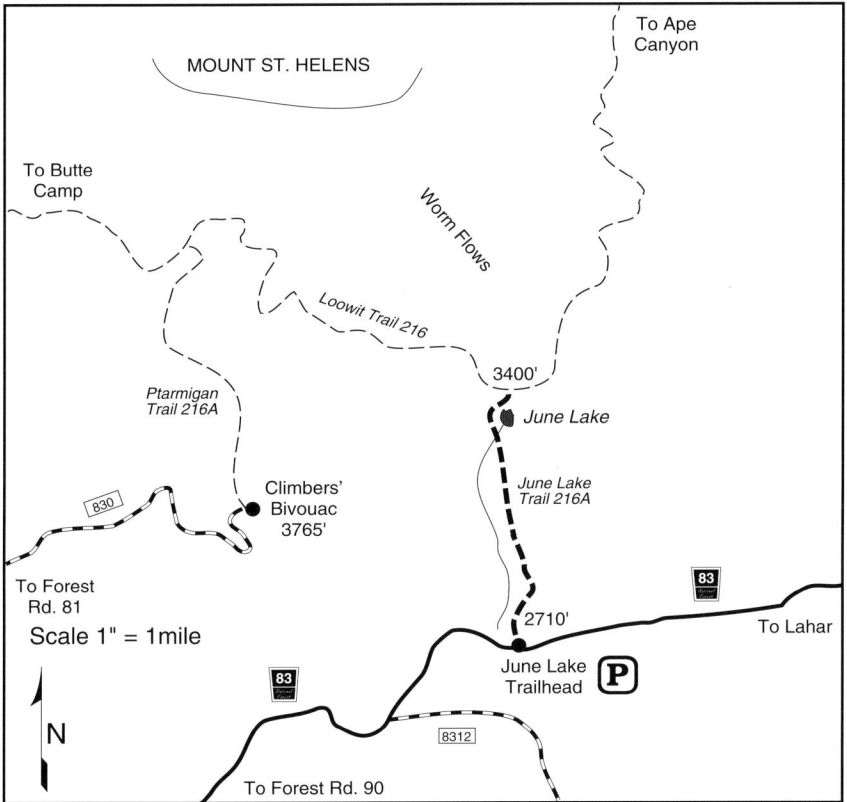

To Ape Canyon

MOUNT ST. HELENS

To Butte Camp

Worm Flows

Loowit Trail 216

3400'

Ptarmigan Trail 216A

June Lake

June Lake Trail 216A

830

Climbers' Bivouac 3765'

To Forest Rd. 81

Scale 1" = 1mile

83

2710'

To Lahar

June Lake Trailhead P

N

83

8312

To Forest Rd. 90

Pine Creek Shelter Trail #216C

—————— Users ——————   Difficulty   ——— Facilities ———

Location: begins, Forest Road 83; ends, lahar
Length: 0.4 miles to the shelter (one way)
Elevation: 2980 feet, low point; 3100 feet, high point
Season: June–November
Use: low

Trail Talk:
• Take a leisurely stroll through a lofty noble fir forest.
• Overlook the Pine Creek drainage scoured clean of vegetation by a
  1980 mudflow.
• Visit the primitive Pine Creek cedar shake shelter built in 1921 and
  restored in 1991.
• Enjoy a stunning view of the lahar and Mount St. Helens' south side
  at the trail's end.
• During winter, blue diamonds mark the route for cross-country skiing
  opportunities.

Trail Facts: This level and maintained trail passes through an old-
growth noble fir forest and then into a clearcut. It reenters the forest,
passes the shelter and terminates at the edge of 1980 mudflow deposits.

Considerations: An excellent short trail for a family outing.

Connections:
• No direct connections.

Map: Mount St. Helens and Smith Creek Butte quadrangles.

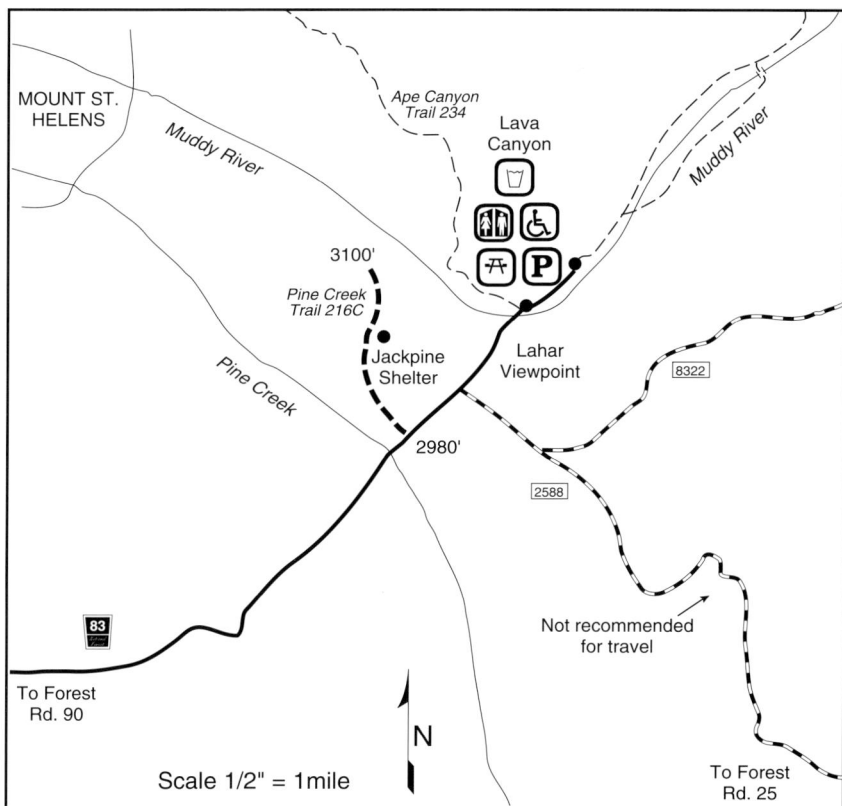

MOUNT ST.
HELENS

Muddy River

Ape Canyon
Trail 234

Lava
Canyon

Muddy River

3100'

Pine Creek
Trail 216C

Jackpine
Shelter

Lahar
Viewpoint

8322

Pine Creek

2980'

2588

83

Not recommended
for travel

To Forest
Rd. 90

N

To Forest
Rd. 25

Scale 1/2" = 1mile

Abraham Trail #216D

——— Users ——— Difficulty ——— Facilities ———

Location: begins, Loowit Trail #216; ends, Truman Trail #207
Length: 2 miles (one way), from Windy Ridge parking lot to Lahar
   10 miles (one way)
Elevation: 4500 feet, high point; 4000 feet, low point
Season: summer to fall
Use: medium

Trail Talk:
• Feel as if you can reach out and touch a living volcano as you hike
  along a ridge that skirts Mount St. Helens' east slope.
• Delight in the wildflowers that return each summer to paint the barren
  hillsides in vibrant colors.
• Look to the east and north and enjoy the views of neighboring
  volcanoes, Mount Adams and Mount Rainier.
• Climb to Windy Pass and look out upon a gray landscape strewn
  with boulders. The Plains of Abraham were created by repeated
  avalanches and mudflows careening off of Mount St. Helens,
  allowing life little chance to take root there.

Trail Facts: The maintained trail climbs a ridgeline until reaching a
steep sand ladder that takes you to Windy Pass. Beyond the pass the
grades become gentler as you cross the Plains of Abraham. The trail
ends at its junction with Loowit Trail #216.

Considerations: There is little shade offered and no potable water.
Come prepared.

Restricted Area: Travel allowed on approved trails only. Off-trail
travel and camping are prohibited to protect sensitive natural features
and scientific studies. Research permits are required for off-trail travel.

Connections:

• Abraham Trail #216 connects with Loowit Trail #216 and by Truman Trail #207.

Map: Spirit Lake East quadrangle.

Windy Trail #216E

────────── Users ────────── Difficulty ────────── Facilities ──────────

Location: begins, Truman Trail #207 (Windy Ridge Trailhead); ends, Loowit Trail #216
Length: 1 mile (one way)
Elevation: 4100 feet, low point; 4340 feet, high point
Season: summer to fall
Use: medium

Trail Talk:
• Gain access to the Loowit Trail #216.
• Enjoy views of Mount St. Helens' eastern slope.
• Cross this harsh, open and rolling terrain which was scoured clean of all vegetation during the 1980 eruption.
• Discover the first pioneering plants to return to the area.

Trail Facts: This maintained trail is accessed by Truman Trail #207 and climbs to its junction with Loowit Trail #216.

Restricted Area: Travel is allowed on approved trails only. Off-trail travel and camping are prohibited to protect sensitive natural features and scientific studies. Research permits are required for off-trail travel.

Connections:
• Windy Trail #216E connects Truman Trail #207 to the Loowit Trail #216, providing access to north and east sections of the Loowit Trail.

Map: Spirit Lake East quadrangle.

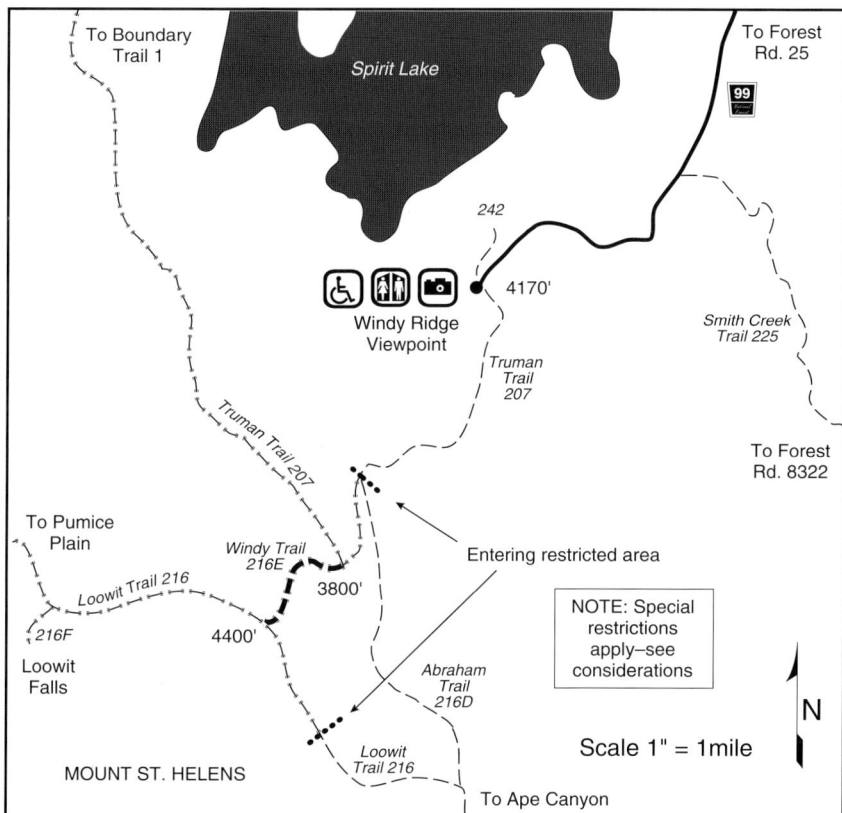

To Boundary Trail 1

Spirit Lake

To Forest Rd. 25

99 Forest Road

242

Windy Ridge Viewpoint

4170'

Truman Trail 207

Smith Creek Trail 225

Truman Trail 207

To Forest Rd. 8322

To Pumice Plain

Windy Trail 216E

Loowit Trail 216

3800'

Entering restricted area

216F

4400'

NOTE: Special restrictions apply–see considerations

Loowit Falls

Abraham Trail 216D

N

MOUNT ST. HELENS

Loowit Trail 216

Scale 1" = 1mile

To Ape Canyon

Castle Ridge Trail #216G

———— Users ———— Difficulty ———— Facilities ————

Location: begins, Weyerhaeuser Road 3000; ends, Loowit Trail #216
Length: 2 miles (one way)
Elevation: 4360 feet, high point; 4000 feet, low point
Season: summer to fall
Use: low

Trail Talk:
• Gain access to Loowit Trail #216 and Castle Lake Trail #221.
• Hike this ridge top and enjoy views of the blast area, Mount St. Helens, the South Fork of the Toutle River, and Castle Lake.
• Excellent elk viewing opportunities abound.

Trail Facts: This intermittently maintained trail follows the ridge top and then terminates at Loowit Trail #216.

Considerations: Weyerhaeuser Road 3000 is extremely difficult to find. Obtain an accurate updated map.

Connections:
• The trail connects with Loowit Trail #216.
• Access to Castle Lake Trail #221 is also provided.

Map: Goat Mountain, Mount St. Helens, Elk Rock, and Spirit Lake West quadrangles.

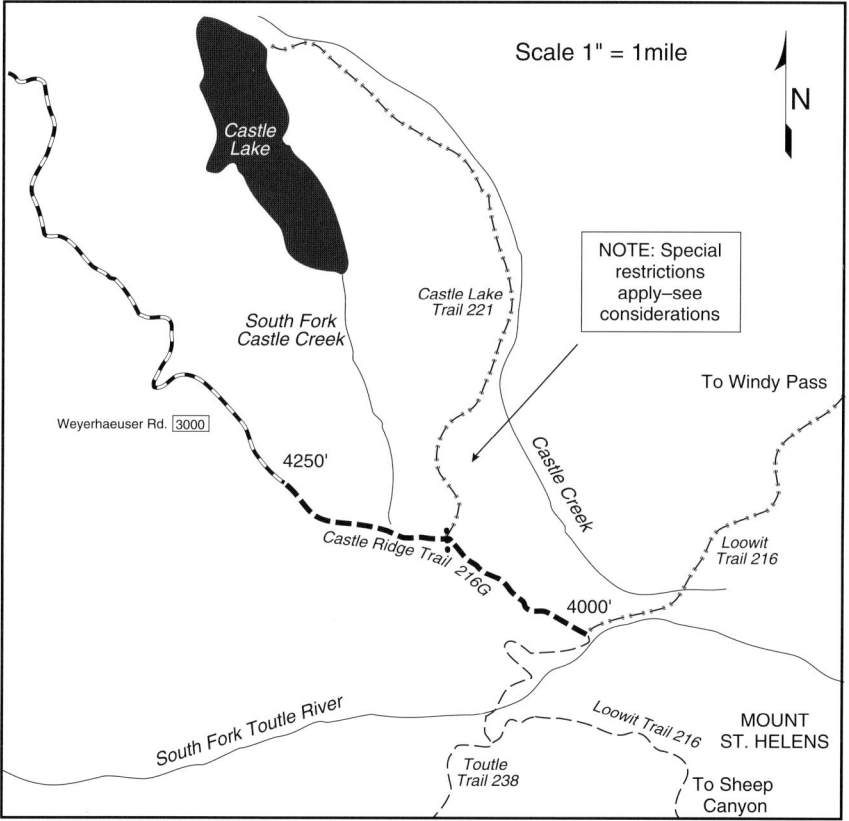

Scale 1" = 1mile

N

Castle Lake

Castle Lake Trail 221

South Fork Castle Creek

NOTE: Special restrictions apply–see considerations

To Windy Pass

Weyerhaeuser Rd. 3000

4250'

Castle Creek

Castle Ridge Trail 216G

Loowit Trail 216

4000'

South Fork Toutle River

Loowit Trail 216

MOUNT ST. HELENS

Toutle Trail 238

To Sheep Canyon

Loowit Trail #216

This exciting trail circles Mount St. Helens, allowing you to experience the entire range of effects the 1980 eruption had on the mountain and the surrounding area. It is a challenging hike across rough terrain. The trail is not crossed by a single road and can be accessed by "feeder" trails identified by the number #216 and a letter of the alphabet, or by Ape Canyon Trail #234, Sheep Canyon Trail #240, and Truman Trail #207. This allows day hikers the opportunity to hike short-distance sections of the trail. These are described in detail in the following pages. The descriptions begin at Butte Camp Trail #238A and continue around the mountain counterclockwise. The entire route is 27 miles in length and each segment varies in its difficulty rating. Campsite opportunities and water availability are limited.

Portions of this trail system enter the Restricted Area. Travel is allowed on approved

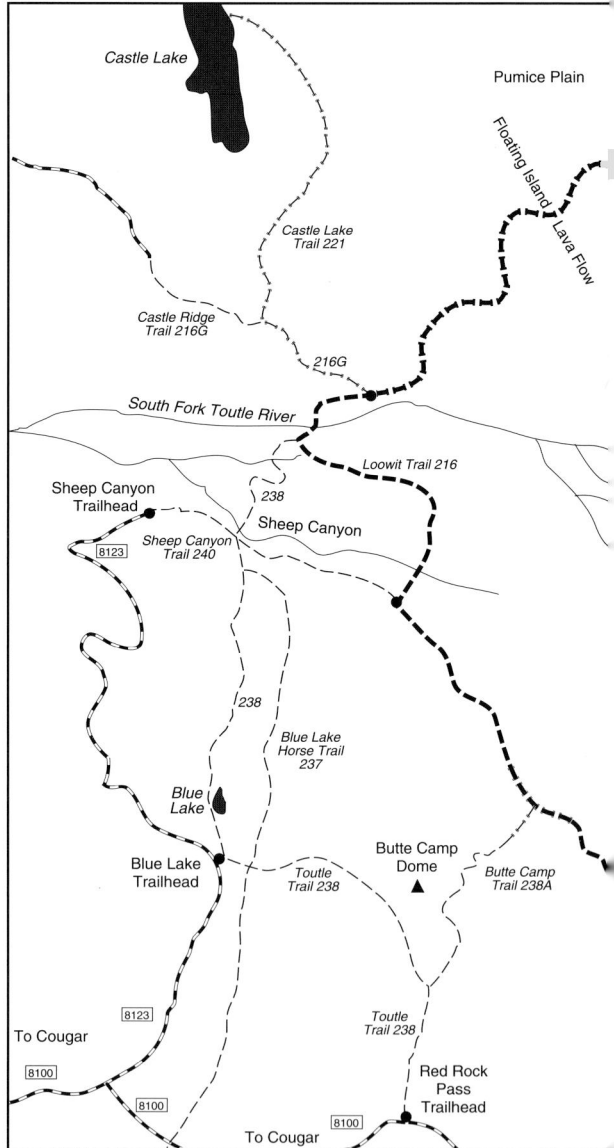

---

trails only. Off-trail travel and camping are prohibited to protect sensitive natural features and scientific studies. Research permits are required for off-trail travel. By planning ahead and coming prepared you will be rewarded with impressive views, new discoveries and a sense of awe of the power of a live volcano.

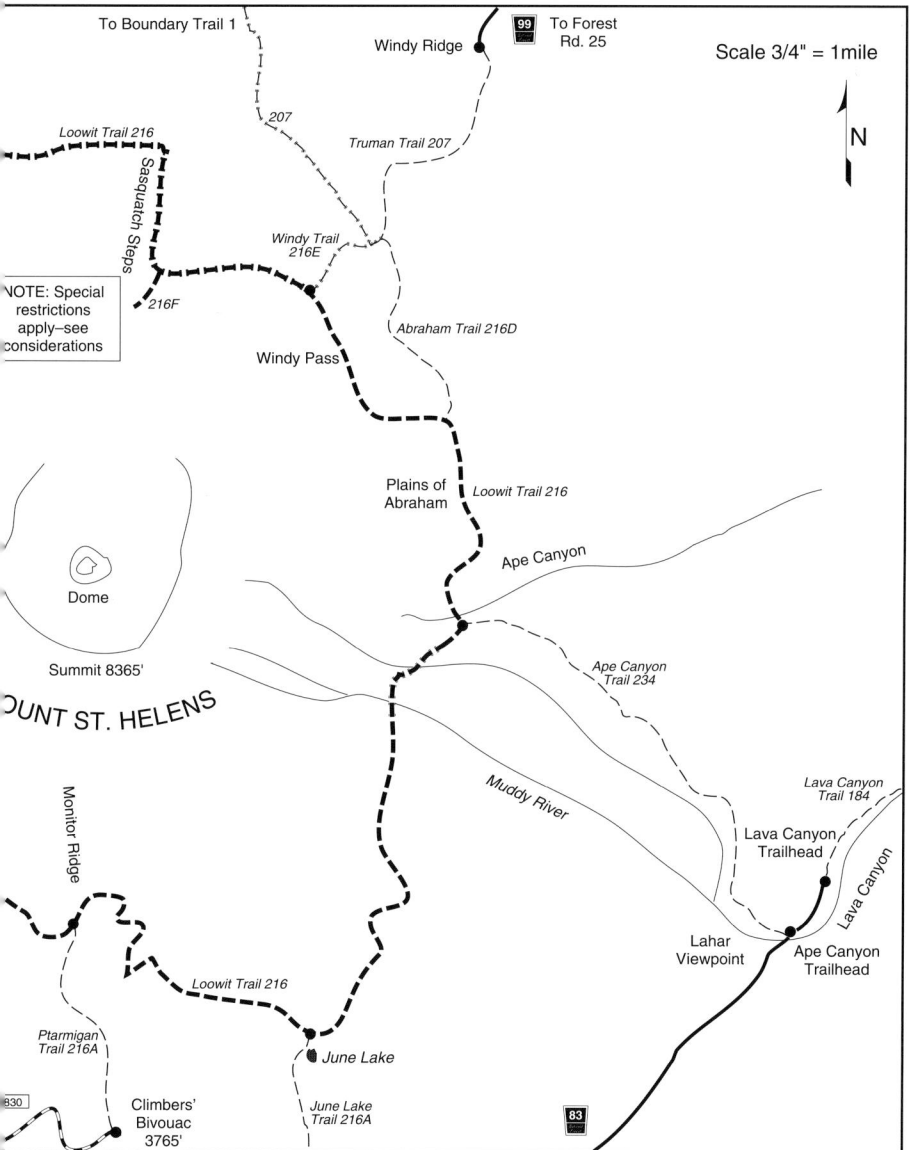

Loowit Trail #216

Butte Camp Trail #238A to Ptarmigan Trail
#216A segment

———— Users ———— Difficulty ———— Facilities ————

Location: begins, Butte Camp Trail #238A; ends, Ptarmigan Trail #216A
Length: 2.2 miles (one way)
Elevation: 4800 feet, high point; 4700 feet, low point
Season: summer to fall
Use: low

Trail Talk:
• Take an invigorating and challenging hike across the rough terrain typical of a young volcano.
• Climb over lava flows reminiscent of rock gardens draped with heather and delicate mosses.
• Enjoy excellent views as you travel along the southern slope of Mount St. Helens.
• Pass through the tall spires of scattered subalpine firs and mountain meadows speckled with wildflowers.
• See the backbone of Monitor Ridge looming larger and larger on the horizon as you near the junction of Ptarmigan Trail #216A.

Trail Facts: This trail receives minimal maintenance and gains little elevation as it follows the timberline of Mount St. Helens. Steep ascents and descents can be expected over massive lava flows. The route is marked by wooden posts over sections with minimal trail tread.

Considerations: Early and late in the season, snowfields can make trail location difficult. There is no potable water available along the trail. This trail is recommended for experienced hikers only.

Restricted Area: Travel is allowed on approved trails only. Off-trail travel and camping are prohibited to protect sensitive natural features and scientific studies. Research permits are required for off-trail travel.

Connections:
• This segment can be accessed by Butte Camp Trail #238A or Ptarmigan Trail #216A.
• It can also be used to approach established climbing routes of Mount St. Helens.

Map: Mount St. Helens quadrangle.

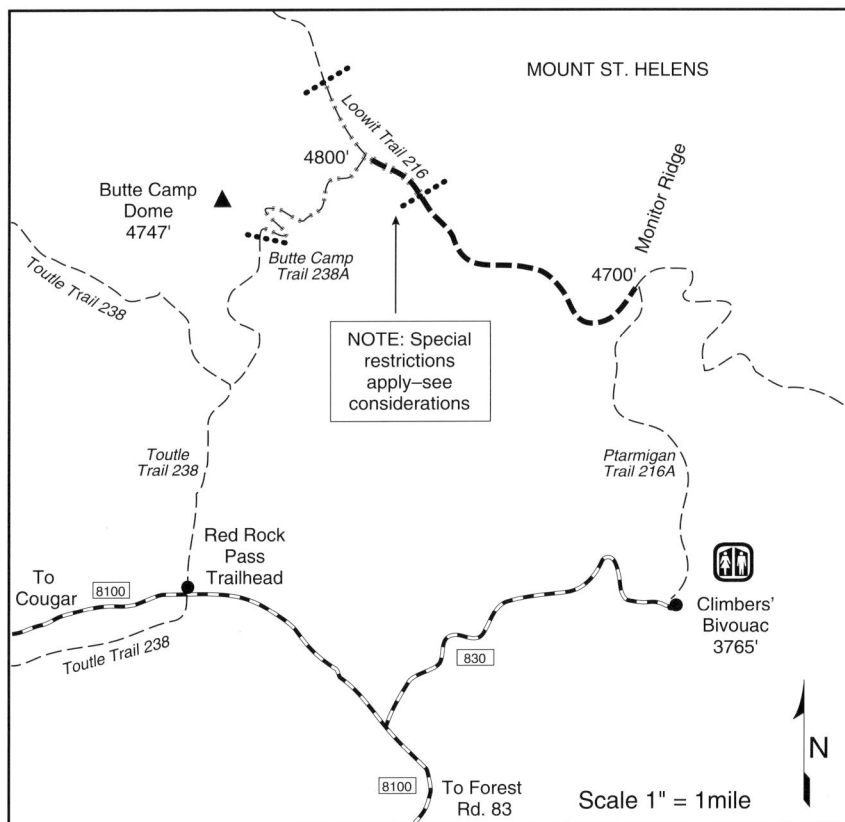

MOUNT ST. HELENS

Loowit Trail 216

4800'

Butte Camp Dome 4747'

Butte Camp Trail 238A

Toutle Trail 238

Monitor Ridge

4700'

NOTE: Special restrictions apply—see considerations

Toutle Trail 238

Ptarmigan Trail 216A

Red Rock Pass Trailhead

To Cougar 8100

Toutle Trail 238

Climbers' Bivouac 3765'

830

8100 To Forest Rd. 83

Scale 1" = 1mile

N

Loowit Trail #216
Ptarmigan Trail #216A to June Lake Trail #216B segment

──── Users ──── Difficulty ──── Facilities ────

Location: begins, Ptarmigan Trail #216A; ends, June Lake Trail #216B
Length: 3.1 miles (one way)
Elevation: 4700 feet, high point; 3400 feet, low point
Season: summer to fall
Use: low

Trail Talk:
• Pass through a subalpine forest setting where you can discover hoop trees. During the 1980 eruption, small saplings were weighted down by heavy ash fall. Their tops remained buried, so they grow in a "hooped over" position.
• Enjoy spectacular views of Mount Adams as you stroll through a vast meadow at timberline's edge.
• Descend into the many-layered canopy of an old-growth forest.
• Ford the snowmelt creek at the crest of Chocolatie Falls. A slurry of rock- and silt-laden waters roll and churn down a 40-foot drop.
• Scramble over the rugged rocks of an ancient lava flow that coursed down the mountain 350 years ago.
• As you near June Lake, pass through trees that have amazingly eluded Mount St. Helens' fury for hundreds of years.

Trail Facts: This low maintenance level trail travels at timberline for most of its route. It passes over the rugged rocky terrain of lava flows and occasionally enters into subalpine or old-growth forest.

Considerations: Water is scarce along the route. Trail location can be difficult, trail is marked by wooden posts and rock cairns. Recommended for experienced hikers only.

Connections:
• This segment can be accessed by Ptarmigan Trail #216A or June Lake Trail #216B.

Map: Mount St. Helens quadrangle.

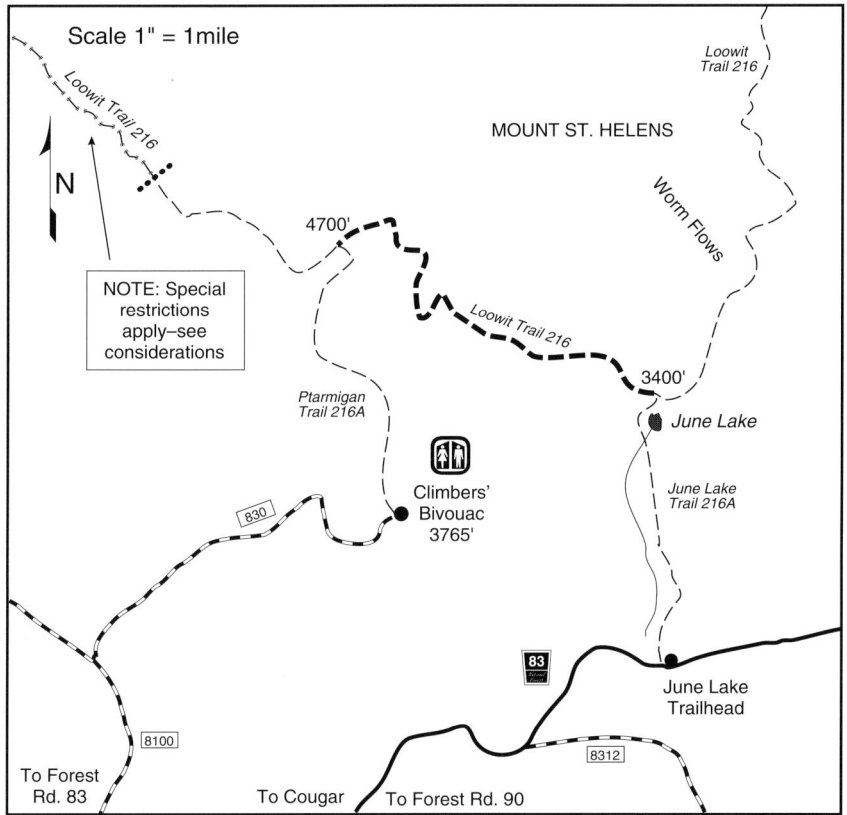

Scale 1" = 1mile

Loowit Trail 216

N

MOUNT ST. HELENS

Loowit Trail 216

Worm Flows

4700'

NOTE: Special
restrictions
apply–see
considerations

Loowit Trail 216

3400'

Ptarmigan
Trail 216A

June Lake

June Lake
Trail 216A

Climbers'
Bivouac
3765'

830

83

June Lake
Trailhead

8100

8312

To Forest
Rd. 83

To Cougar

To Forest Rd. 90

Loowit Trail #216

*June Lake Trail #216B to Ape Canyon
Trail #234 segment*

———— Users ———— Difficulty ———— Facilities ————

Location: begins, June Lake Trail #216B; ends, Ape Canyon
Length: 4.7 miles (one way)
Elevation: 3400 feet, low point; 4200 feet, high point
Season: summer to fall
Use: low

Trail Talk:

• Be rewarded on this challenging high-elevation hike by the constantly changing terrain offered by the volcanic landscape.
• Pass beneath majestic towering trees that have stood as sentinels at Mount St. Helens' base for over 200 years.
• Discover the miniature valley of Short Creek. The creek suddenly appears and disappears beneath a lava flow and then continues on its way to plunge over a basalt cliff into June Lake.
• Traverse around the jagged toe of the Worm Flows at the forest edge.
• Break out into a raw and rugged landscape as you near the lahar. Cross steep gullies at the headwaters of Pine Creek and the Muddy River as Mount St. Helens looms silently and ominously overhead.

Trail Facts: This minimally maintained, rugged mountain trail crosses an area that is of great geologic interest. Sections of this trail are steep scrambles across loose rocky slopes and drainages. In places the trail location is identified by wooden post route markers.

Considerations: Safe crossing of drainages may change as seasonal storms remove sections of the trail. Water is scarce along this trail. Recommended for experienced hikers only.

Restricted Area: Travel is allowed on approved trails only. Off-trail travel and camping are prohibited to protect sensitive natural features and scientific studies. Research permits are required for off-trail travel.

Connections:
• This segment connects with the Ape Canyon Trail #234 at Ape Canyon.
• The trail can be accessed from June Lake Trail #216B.

Map: Mount St. Helens and Smith Creek Butte quadrangle.

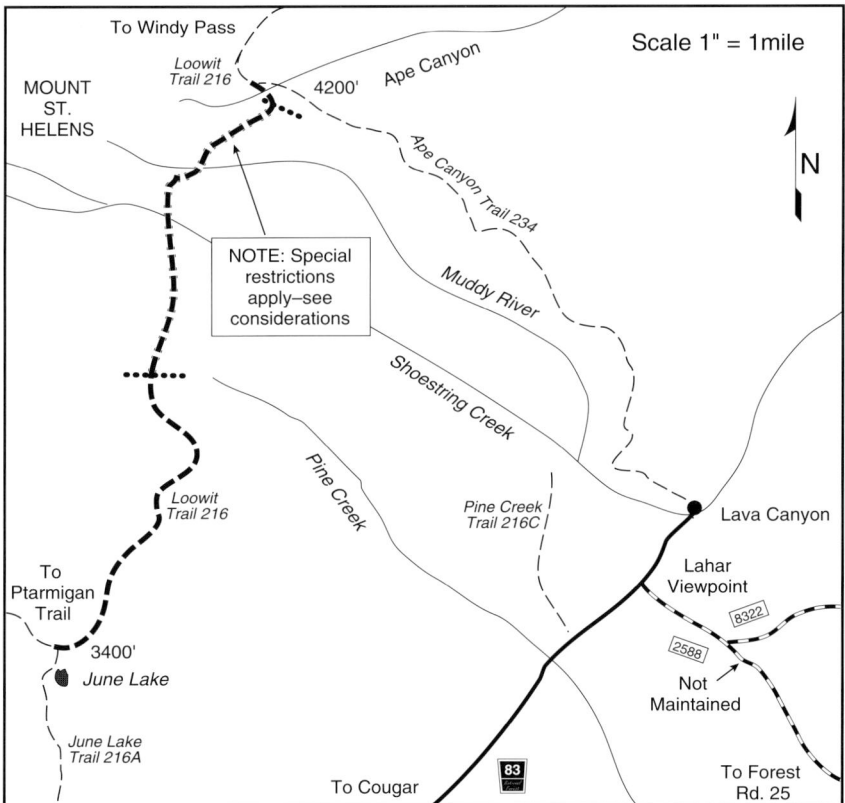

To Windy Pass

Loowit Trail 216

Ape Canyon

Scale 1" = 1mile

MOUNT ST. HELENS

4200'

Ape Canyon Trail 234

N

NOTE: Special restrictions apply–see considerations

Muddy River

Shoestring Creek

Pine Creek

Loowit Trail 216

Pine Creek Trail 216C

Lava Canyon

To Ptarmigan Trail

Lahar Viewpoint

8322

2588

3400'

June Lake

Not Maintained

June Lake Trail 216A

To Cougar

83

To Forest Rd. 25

Loowit Trail #216

Ape Canyon Trail #234 to Windy Trail
#216E segment

———— Users ———— Difficulty ———— Facilities ————

Location: begins, Ape Canyon Trail #234; ends, Windy Trail #216E
Length: 3.7 miles (one way)
Elevation: 4200 feet, low point; 4850 feet, high point
Season: summer to fall
Use: low

Trail Talk:
• Wind around the east side of Mount St. Helens and enjoy views of the surrounding area.
• Travel over Windy Pass and then descend to the Pumice Plain.
• View miles of landscape transformed by the power of a volcanic eruption.

Trail Facts: This intermittently maintained trail traverses the east side of Mount St. Helens. In places the trail location is identified by wooden post route markers and rock cairns.

Considerations: Water is scarce along this route. Mountain bike use is allowed on the segment of #216 from Ape Canyon to the junction of Abraham Trail #216D.

Restricted Area: Travel is allowed on approved trails only. Off-trail travel and camping are prohibited to protect sensitive natural features and scientific studies. Research permits are required for off-trail travel.

Connection:
• Ape Canyon Trail #234 provides access to this section of the Loowit Trail.
• Windy Trail #216E connects Truman Trail #207 to Loowit Trail #216.

Map: Mount St. Helens and Smith Creek Butte quadrangles.

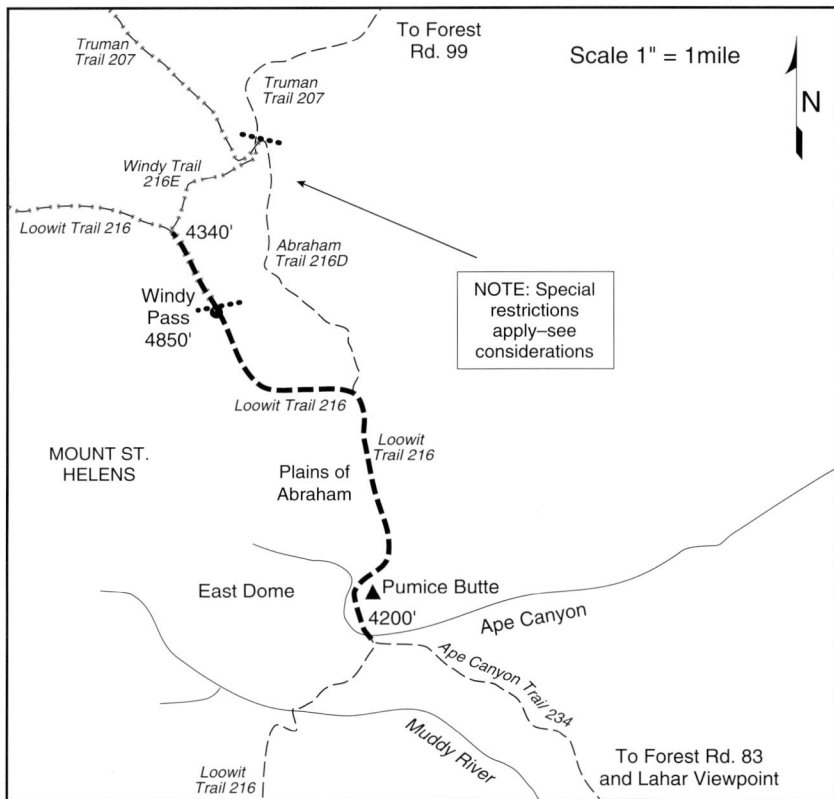

Loowit Trail #216

Windy Trail #216E to Castle Ridge
Trail #216G

———— Users ———— Difficulty ———— Facilities ————

Location: begins, Windy Trail #216E; ends, Castle Ridge Trail
   #216G
Length: 7.8 miles (one way)
Elevation: 4560 feet, high point; 3800 feet, low point
Season: summer to fall
Use: low

Trail Talk:
• Hike into the very heart of the blast zone.
• Discover how a debris avalanche, a pyroclastic flow and a mudflow
  transformed the features of the area forever.
• Obtain views of Loowit Falls and the steaming dome and crater of
  Mount St. Helens.
• Learn about the important research taking place that enables scientists
  to unlock many of the mysteries surrounding volcanic eruptions.

Trail Facts: This intermittently maintained trail traverses the pumice
plain and broken terrain in front of Mount St. Helens. The trail is
subject to washouts. The route is marked by wooden posts and rock
cairns.

Considerations: Water is scarce along this route. Trail is often
difficult to locate, especially in inclement weather.

Restricted Area: Travel is allowed on approved trails only. Off-trail
travel and camping are prohibited to protect sensitive natural features
and scientific studies. Research permits are required for off-trail travel.

Connections:
• This segment can be accessed from Windy Trail #216E via Truman
  #207 and Castle Ridge Trail #216G.

Map: Mount St. Helens quadrangle.

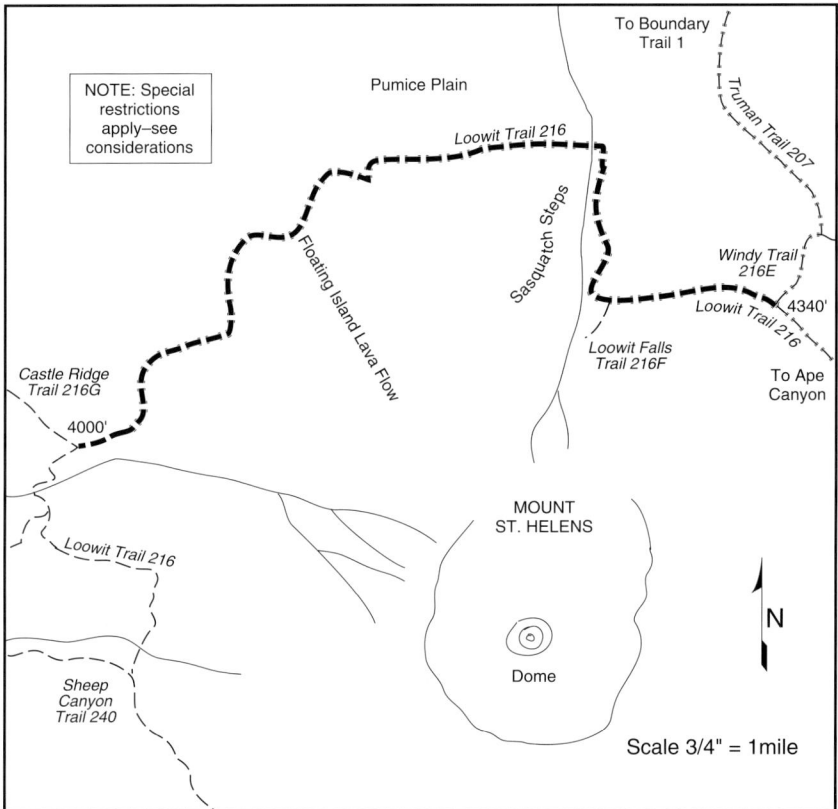

Loowit Trail #216

Castle Ridge Trail #216G Segment to
Sheep Canyon Trail #240

———— Users ————   Difficulty   ———— Facilities ————

Location: begins, Castle Ridge Trail #216G; ends, Sheep Canyon
     Trail #240
Length: 2.0 miles (one way)
Elevation: 3250 feet, low point; 4700 feet, high point
Season: summer to fall
Use: low

Trail Talk:
- Few trails capture more completely the range of effects of the 1980 eruption. Discover views of mudflow-scoured river valleys, blast-singed trees, miles of blown-down forest, and views of newly created lakes on this segment of the Loowit Trail.
- Understand by closely observing this raw landscape how the familiar features of the Cascade Range were formed.
- Walk out onto a huge boulder and enjoy an impressive view of the headwall of the South Fork of the Toutle River.
- Scan the horizon for outstanding views of Mount St. Helens, Mount Margaret, Mount Rainier and Johnston Ridge. Also enjoy the view of newly created Coldwater Lake.
- Descend to the South Fork of the Toutle River. This once well-forested valley was transformed into the skeletal remains of ash-covered logs and shattered stumps by the fury of a fiery blast of fragmented rock and the abrasive action of a raging mudflow.

Trail Facts: From the heart of the blast area, this maintained trail descends into the Pumice Bowl and crosses via ford the South Fork Toutle River and climbs through a subalpine environment to panoramic views as it traverses the ridge.

Considerations: Beware of the steep slopes near Sheep Canyon and the Pumice Bowl (above the South Fork Toutle River). Rockfall can obscure the trail and make your footing treacherous. For an excellent day loop trail, see "connections" under Sheep Canyon Trail #240. Take care to preserve fragile vegetation by staying on the trail.

Connections:
• This section can be accessed by Sheep Canyon Trail #240, Toutle Trail #238, and Castle Ridge Trail #216G.

Map: Goat Mountain and Mount St. Helens quadrangle.

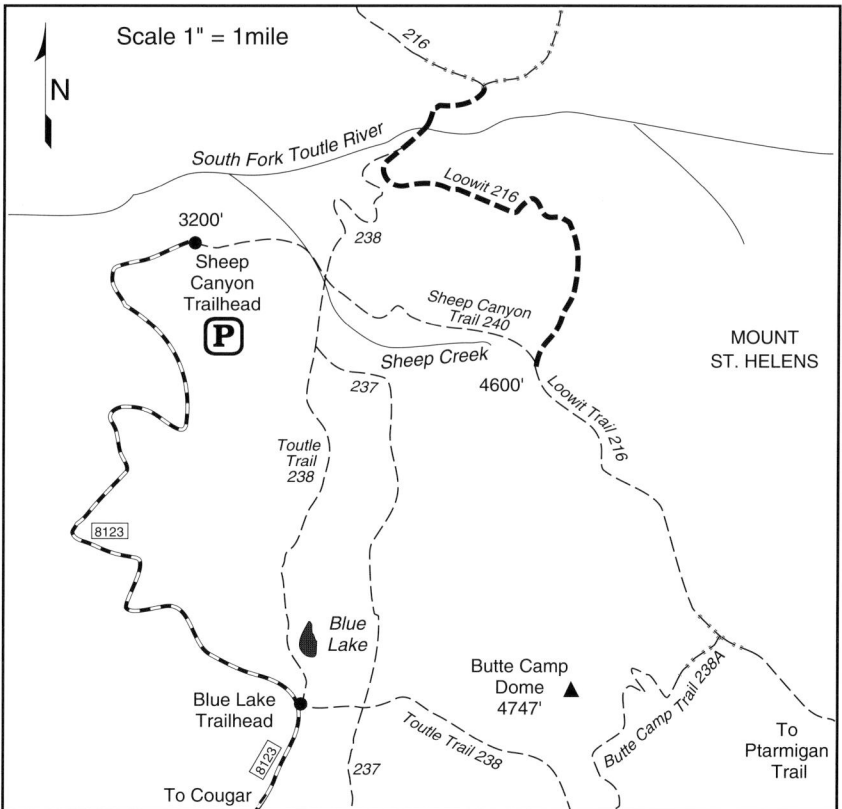

Loowit Trail #216

*Sheep Canyon Trail #240 to Butte Camp
#238A Segment*

——————— Users ——————— Difficulty ——————— Facilities ———————

Location: begins, Sheep Canyon Trail #240; ends, Butte Camp Trail #238A
Length: 3 miles (one way)
Elevation: 4700 feet, low point; 4800 feet, high point
Season: summer to fall
Use: low

Trail Talk:
- Weave in and out of timberline as you skirt Mount St. Helens' western slope.
- Cross large glacial canyons and avalanche chutes that are more typical of Mount Rainier or Mount Adams, the Cascades' "older and more weathered" volcanoes.
- Enjoy the beauty of subalpine settings and a bounty of wildflowers during the summer season.
- Explore numerous mudflows and the rugged jumble of rock from past lava flows.
- Protect the fragile meadow of Upper Butte Camp where important plant succession research is taking place.
- Survey the panorama to the south and east where you'll discover views of Mount Hood, Mount Adams, Yale Reservoir and the Lewis River Valley.

Trail Facts: This trail receives minimal maintenance and traverses the western slope of the mountain, connecting Sheep Canyon Trail #240 to Butte Camp Trail #238A. It gains little elevation on the route, descending and ascending steeply only out of the glaciated valleys.

Considerations: Minimum maintenance and snows early or late in the season could make this trail's rating "most difficult." During the hot summer months no water is available and the trail offers little shade.

Restricted Area: Travel is allowed on approved trails only. Off-trail travel and camping are prohibited to protect sensitive natural features and scientific studies. Research permits are required for off-trail travel.

Connections:
• This segment can be accessed by Sheep Canyon Trail #240 or Butte Camp #238A.

Map: Goat Mountain and Mount St. Helens quadrangle.

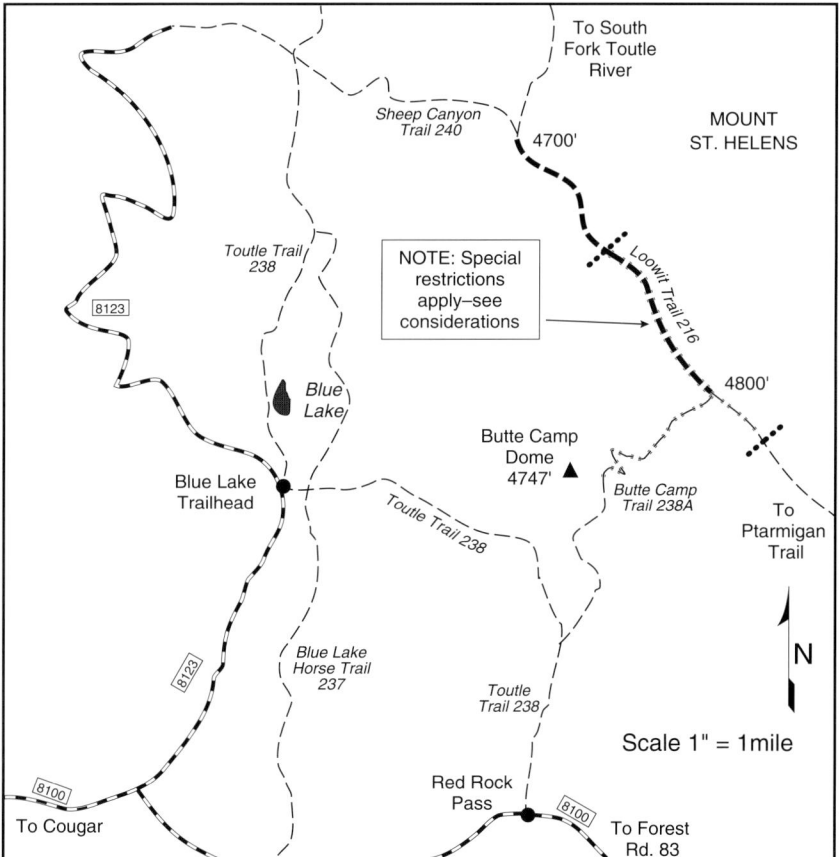

Goat Mountain Trail #217

and Vanson Peak Trail #217A

———— Users ———— Difficulty ———— Facilities ————

Location: begins, Goat Mountain Trailhead, Forest Road 2612; ends, Weyerhaeuser Road 2600

Length: 10 miles (one way); Vanson Peak 1.4 miles (one way)

Elevation: 2500 feet, low point; 5100 feet, high point; 3900 feet, mid point

Season: summer to fall

Use: low

Trail Talk:

• From the trailhead enjoy an exhilarating hike through the blast area, to the alpine terrain of Goat Mountain.

• Cross and recross the thin line that meant life or death on May 18th, 1980, as you weave in and out of the living green forest and the standing dead trees that mark the outer edge of the blast zone.

• Discover sparkling spring-fed ponds cradled in grassy basins that lie far below the trail.

• Rest at forest-enveloped Deadmans Lake. The crystal blue waters provide a beautiful setting for a base camp.

• Climb the crest of Goat Mountain where you can gaze across forested hillsides until they meet with formidable Mount Rainier.

• To the south, Mount St. Helens' shadowy form towers amidst a sea of ashen gray mudflows, avalanche debris, stumps and logs.

• Pass through wildflower-sprinkled meadows that arch across the skyline.

• Descend into an evergreen forest as you make your way to the northern trailhead.

• For further exploration take the side trip to Vanson Peak or stop for a refreshing break at Vanson Lake.

Trail Facts: This maintained trail passes through a portion of the blast zone where the timber was salvaged near Ryan Lake. It then climbs via switchbacks to the crest of Goat Mountain, then descends to Deadmans

Lake. Climbing from the lake, it enters more alpine terrain and junctions with the side trail to Vanson Peak or continues at a steep descent to Vanson Lake. It ends at Weyerhaeuser Road 2600.

Considerations: Preserve the beauty of this remote alpine setting by using low-impact camping methods.

Connections:
• Near Deadmans Lake, Tumwater Trail #218 heads to the northeast. Side trails to Vanson Peak and Vanson Lake are accessed on the northern section of trail.
• Vanson Ridge Trail #213A connects the Goat Mountain Trail to the Green River Trail #213.

Map: Cowlitz Falls and Vanson Peak quadrangles.

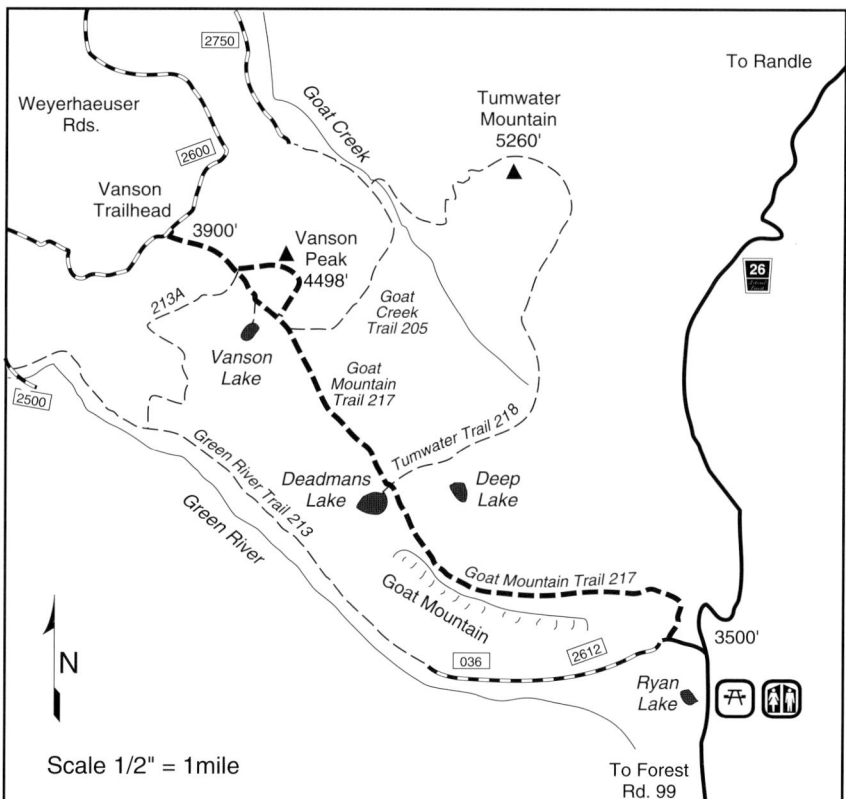

Tumwater Trail #218

——— Users ———   Difficulty   ——— Facilities ———

Location: begins, Goat Mountain Trail #217; ends, Tumwater Mountain
Length: 9.0 miles (one way)
Elevation: 4352 feet, low point; 4800 feet, high point
Season: summer to fall
Use: low

Trail Talk:
• Hike the razorback ridge of Tumwater Mountain which provides you
  with spectacular views of forested drainages and Cascade volcanoes.
• Enjoy views of the pristine Goat Creek drainage.
• Identify wildflowers where the forest gives way to rocky outcrops.
• Find solitude in this remote setting.
• Reach the rocky summit of Tumwater Mountain.
• Discover a small snowmelt pond set in a meadow at the base of
  Tumwater Mountain.

Trail Facts: This maintained trail takes off from Goat Mountain Trail
#217 near Deadmans Lake. It climbs steadily until reaching the summit
of Tumwater Mountain.

Considerations: Water should be treated for safe drinking. No water
is available between Deadmans Lake and Tumwater Mountain.

Map: Cowlitz Falls and Vanson Peak quadrangles.

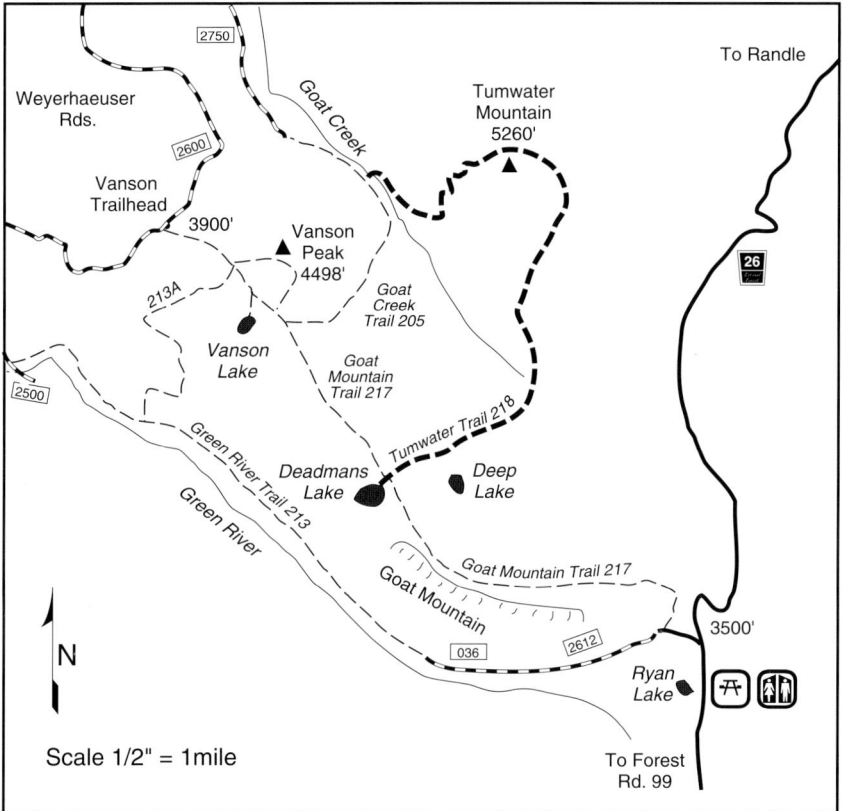

To Randle

2750

Goat Creek

Tumwater
Mountain
5260'

Weyerhaeuser
Rds.

2600

26

Vanson
Trailhead

3900'

Vanson
Peak
4498'

213A

Goat
Creek
Trail 205

Vanson
Lake

Goat
Mountain
Trail 217

2500

Green River Trail 213

Tumwater Trail 218

Green River

Deadmans
Lake

Deep
Lake

Goat Mountain Trail 217

Goat Mountain

036

2612

3500'

N

Ryan
Lake

Scale 1/2" = 1mile

To Forest
Rd. 99

Strawberry Mtn. Trail #220

——— Users ——— Difficulty ——— Facilities ———

Location: begins, on Road 2600; ends, Boundary Trail #1 near Bear Meadow
Length: 10.7 miles (one way)
Elevation: 2400 feet, low point; 5600 feet, high point
Season: July–October
Use: moderate

Trail Talk:
• Enjoy spectacular views of Mount St. Helens and the blanket of blown-down forest in the valley below as the trail skirts the edge of the blast zone from the May 18, 1980 eruption.
• Discover the beauty and complexity of the fragile high-elevation ecology.

Trail Facts: The trail climbs steeply through thick forest up to Strawberry Mountain. It then traverses the semi-open ridge top. The trail crosses Forest Road 2516 where it junctions with a short side trail to the old lookout site on top of Strawberry Mountain. It then continues south, descending to junction with the Boundary Trail #1 near Bear Meadow.

Considerations: The trail ascends steeply in the first 3 miles. Be prepared to share the trail with hikers, horses and mountain bikes.

Connections: Strawberry Mountain Trail #220 connects with Boundary Trail #1 near Bear Meadow. Horse travel is prohibited for Boundary Trail #1 west of Bear Meadow.

Map: Cowlitz Falls and Vanson Peak quadrangles.

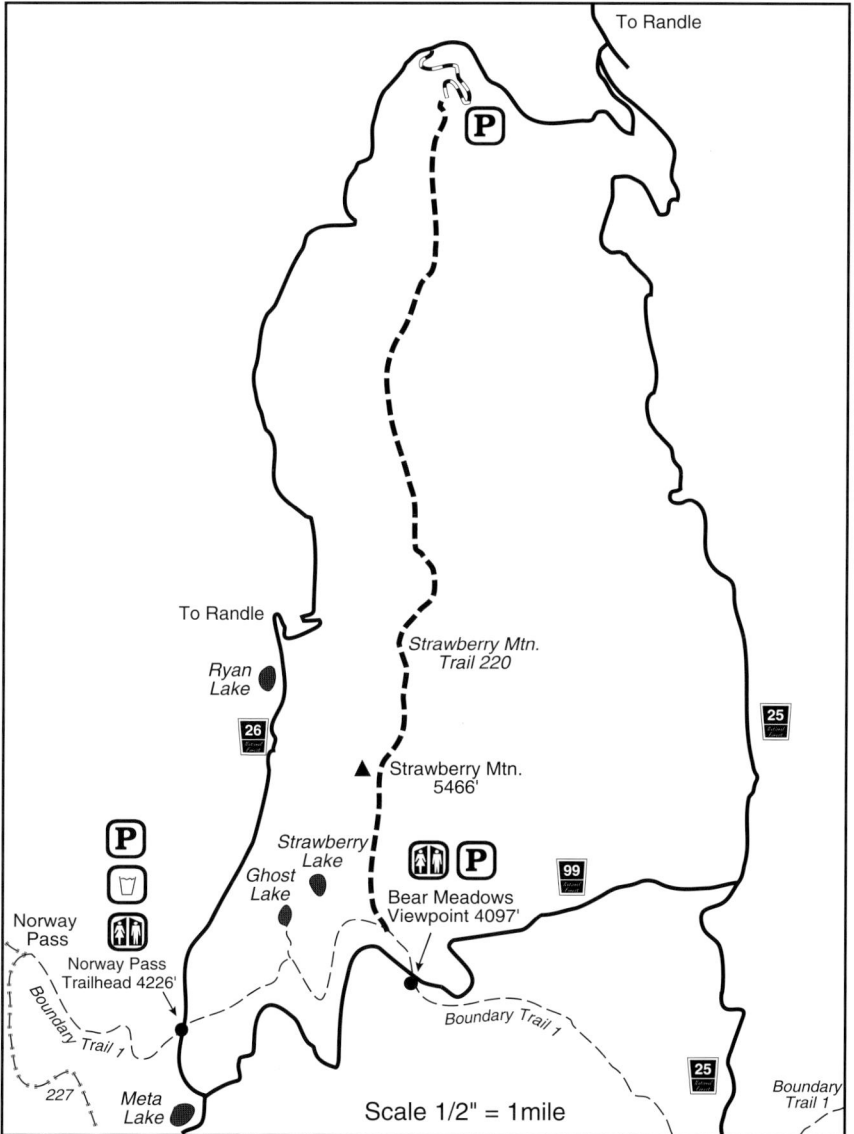

To Randle

P

To Randle

Ryan
Lake

*Strawberry Mtn.
Trail 220*

26

25

▲ Strawberry Mtn.
5466'

P

Strawberry
Lake

Ghost
Lake

Bear Meadows
Viewpoint 4097'

99

Norway
Pass

P

Norway Pass
Trailhead 4226'

Boundary Trail 1

Boundary Trail 1

227

Meta
Lake

25

*Boundary
Trail 1*

Scale 1/2" = 1mile

Castle Lake Trail #221

——— Users ——— Difficulty ——— Facilities ———

Location: begins, Castle Ridge Trail #216G; ends, Castle Lake
Length: 4 miles (one way)
Elevation: 4280 feet, high point; 2510 feet, low point
Season:summer to fall
Use: low

Trail Talk:
• Take a pleasant side trip off of Castle Ridge Trail #216G to view
  Castle Lake. Castle Lake was created when the debris avalanche
  dammed South Fork Castle Creek.
• Obtain excellent views of Mount St. Helens.
• Parallel Castle Creek passing through boggy areas that are teeming
  with wildlife.
• Experience the immense magnitude of the 1980 eruption as you dis-
  cover the effects of the debris avalanche.
• Enjoy the scenic setting of Castle Lake.

Trail Facts: This minimally maintained trail climbs the ridge, then
drops down and follows Castle Creek to Castle Lake.

Considerations: Protect the fragile ecosystem by using low-impact
camping methods.

Restricted Area: Travel allowed on approved trails only. Off-trail
travel and camping are prohibited to protect sensitive natural features
and scientific studies. Research permits are required for off-trail travel.

Connections:
• Castle Ridge Trail #216G connects the Castle Lake Trail to Loowit
  Trail #216.

Map: Goat Mountain, Mount St. Helens, Elk Rock, and Spirit Lake West quadrangles.

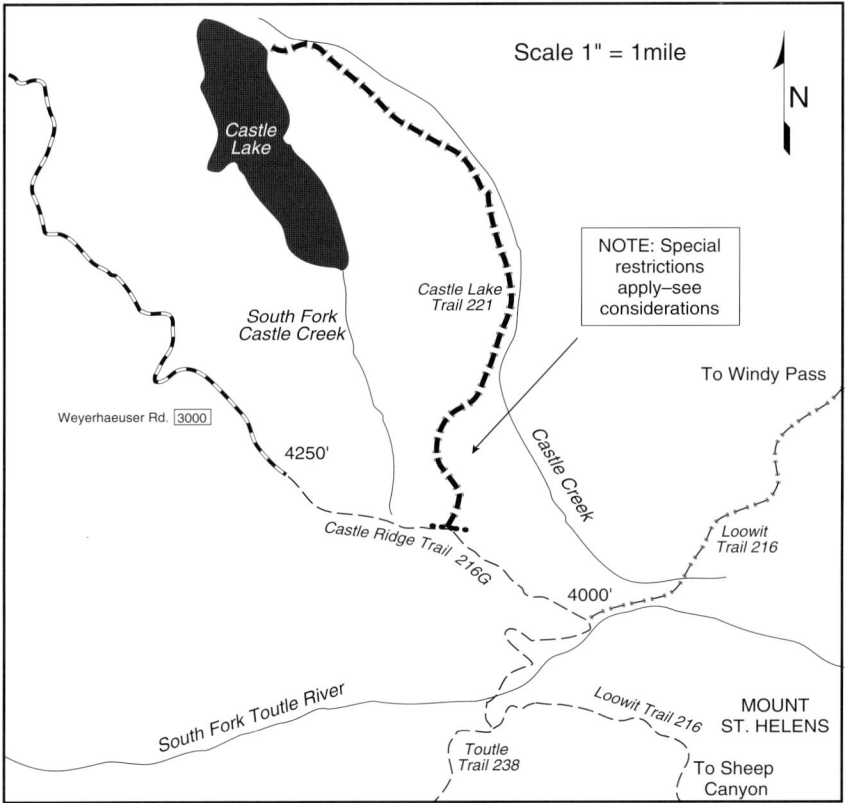

Scale 1" = 1mile

N

Castle Lake

Castle Lake Trail 221

South Fork Castle Creek

NOTE: Special restrictions apply–see considerations

To Windy Pass

Weyerhaeuser Rd. 3000

4250'

Castle Creek

Loowit Trail 216

Castle Ridge Trail 216G

4000'

South Fork Toutle River

Loowit Trail 216

MOUNT ST. HELENS

Toutle Trail 238

To Sheep Canyon

Harmony Trail #224

——————— Users ——————— Difficulty ———— Facilities ————

Location: begins, Harmony Viewpoint, Forest Road 99; ends, Spirit Lake
Length: 1.0 mile (one way)
Elevation: 4000 feet, high point; 3400 feet, low point
Season: summer to fall
Use: high

Trail Talk:
• Through an interpretive sign, you can share in the memories of the people who once came to vacation at rustic Harmony Falls Lodge and fell in love with the timeless beauty of Spirit Lake and Mount St. Helens.
• Imagine the morning of May 18, 1980, when a lateral blast of abrasive winds and searing gases rolled along these ridges, toppling the forest in its path.
• Envision a massive avalanche sliding off of Mount St. Helens, plummeting into Spirit Lake and creating a gigantic wave, sweeping the hillside of the newly blown-down trees.
• Discover what remains of Harmony Falls. The rest lies buried beneath an enlarged lake which floats upon the shattered mountaintop.
• Gaze into the crystal waters which yesterday reflected a tranquil way of life and today mirror a world of change.

Trail Facts: This maintained trail descends steeply along the north side of the ridge overlooking Spirit Lake. It provides the only access to the lake at this time. The trail ends at the shoreline. The views of Mount St. Helens, the crater, the lava dome and Spirit Lake are outstanding.

Considerations: The trail quickly drops 600 feet in elevation. Be prepared for the climb back up. Caution should be used along the shoreline; dropoffs are steep, and the shifting logs dangerous!

Restricted Area: Travel is allowed on approved trails only. Off-trail travel and camping are prohibited to protect sensitive natural features and scientific studies. Research permits are required for off-trail travel.

Connections:
• Harmony Trail #224 is one of many trails exploring the blast area along Forest Road 99. Other nearby trails include Meta Lake Trail #210, Independence Pass Trail #227 and Windy Ridge Sand Ladder Trail #242. There are no direct trail connections.

Map: Spirit Lake West and Spirit Lake East quadrangles.

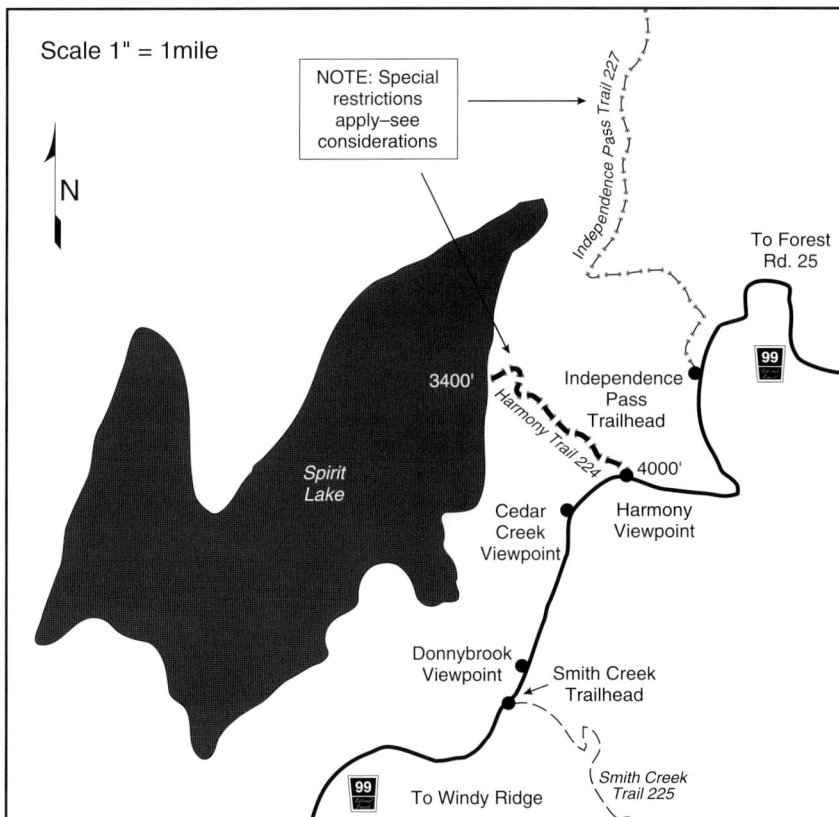

Smith Creek Trail #225

———— Users ———— Difficulty ——— Facilities ————

Location: begins, Smith Creek Trailhead, Forest Road 99; ends,
  Smith Creek Trailhead Forest Road 8322
Length: 9 miles (one way)
Elevation: 4080 feet, high point; 1575 feet, low point
Season: summer to fall
Use: low

Trail Talk:
• Marvel at the immense impact the eruption of Mount St. Helens had
  on the Smith Creek drainage.
• Hike through miles of blast area and discover masses of logs carried
  by mudflows to their resting place along the river.
• Notice the healing landscape.
• Enjoy distant views of waterfalls as they plunge off rocky cliffs.

Trail Facts: This maintained trail follows the Smith Creek drainage.
It descends steadily from Forest Road 99 to Smith Creek. It follows old
sections of road and crosses open sections that are marked by wooden
post route markers. The trail crosses the Muddy River via a bridge and
ends at the lower Smith Creek Trailhead on Forest Road 8322.

Considerations: Pay attention to trail markers as it is easy to miss
them. The trail provides little shade. Come prepared with plenty of
water (water is available but should be treated for safe drinking).

Connections:
• Smith Creek Trail #225 connects with Lava Canyon Trail #184 near
  its lower trailhead.

Map: Smith Creek Butte quadrangle.

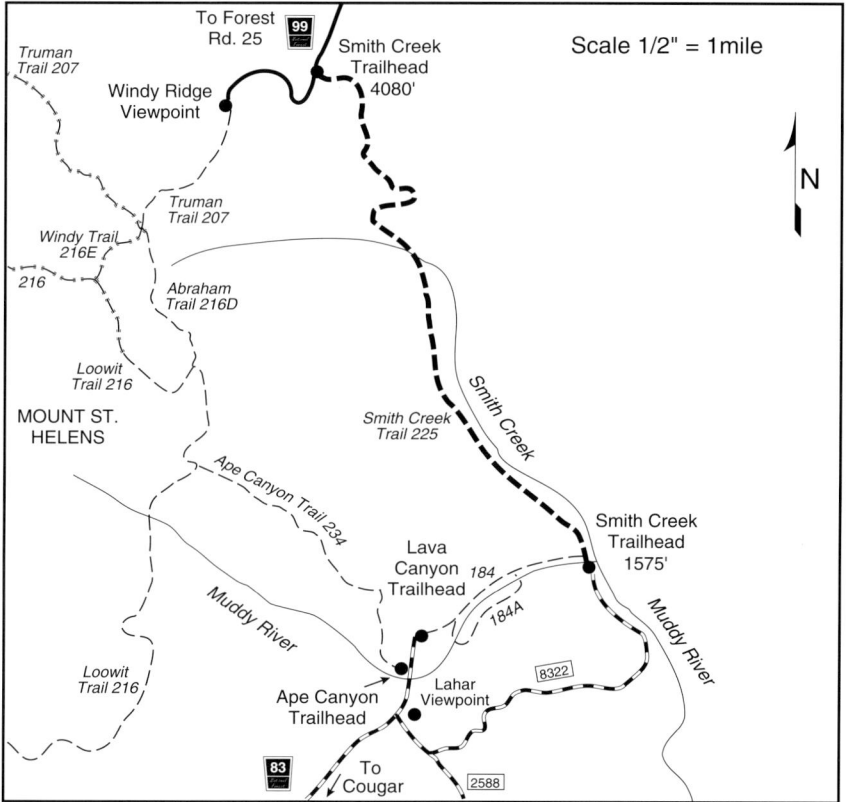

To Forest Rd. 25

99

Truman Trail 207

Smith Creek Trailhead 4080'

Windy Ridge Viewpoint

Scale 1/2" = 1mile

N

Truman Trail 207

Windy Trail 216E

216

Abraham Trail 216D

Loowit Trail 216

MOUNT ST. HELENS

Smith Creek Trail 225

Smith Creek

Ape Canyon Trail 234

Smith Creek Trailhead 1575'

Lava Canyon Trailhead

184

184A

Muddy River

Muddy River

Loowit Trail 216

Ape Canyon Trailhead

Lahar Viewpoint

8322

83

To Cougar

2588

Independence Pass Trail #227

———— Users ———— Difficulty ———— Facilities ————

P

Location: begins, Independence Pass Viewpoint, Forest Road 99;
    ends, Norway Pass on Boundary Trail #1
Length: 3.5 miles (one way)
Elevation: 4000 feet, low point; 4500 feet, high point
Season: summer to early fall
Use: medium

Trail Talk:
• Take a short hike (1/4 mile) and be rewarded with a striking view of
  Mount St. Helens, the crater, the lava dome and Spirit Lake.
• Witness the dramatic change in landscape that offers new insights
  into the dynamic nature of our planet.
• Be amazed at the rapid return of life to this once gray and seemingly
  bleak land.
• Exploring further, discover towering rock pinnacles uncloaked by the
  shattering force of the lateral blast.
• Enjoy unsurpassed views of a living laboratory where the earth's
  wondrous process of geological change is unfolding before our eyes.

Trail Facts: This maintained trail ascends a ridge for 1/4 of a mile, offering excellent views in all directions. It continues north through the blast zone. After 1.5 miles there is a superb overlook of Spirit Lake and excellent views into the crater and dome. Beyond this point the trail narrows and passes imposing rock pinnacles and then continues on to the junction with the Boundary Trail #1 at Norway Pass.

Considerations: No water is available on this trail and little shade is offered. The trail is subject to washouts beyond 1.5 miles.

Restricted Area: Travel is allowed on approved trails only. Off-trail travel and camping are prohibited to protect sensitive natural features and scientific studies. Research permits are required for off-trail travel.

Connections:
• Independence Pass Trail #227 is one of the many trails accessed from Road 99 that explore the blast area. Others include Meta Lake Trail #210, Harmony Trail #224, Windy Ridge Sand Ladder #242, and Boundary Trail #1.
• The trail ties directly into the Boundary Trail #1 at Norway Pass.

Map: Spirit Lake East and Spirit Lake West quadrangle.

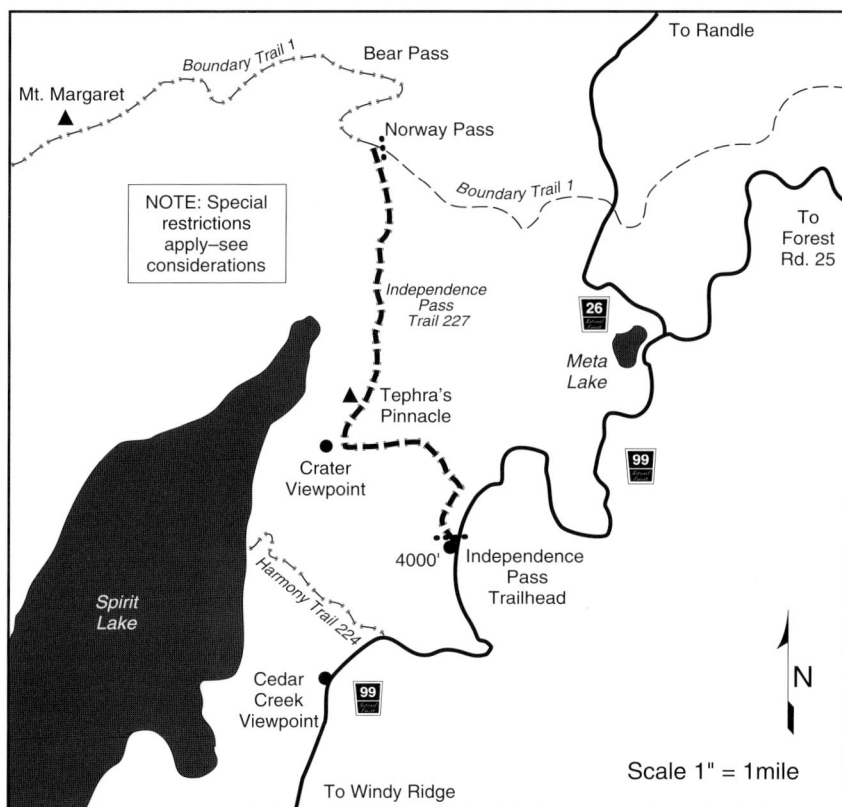

Coldwater Trail #230

─────── Users ───────   Difficulty   ─────── Facilities ───────

Location: begins, Boundary Trail #1; ends Lakes Trail #211.
Length: 4.5 miles (one way)
Elevation: 5200 feet, high point; 2800 feet, low point
Season: summer to fall
Use: low

Trail Talk:
• Enjoy spectacular views of Mount St. Helens, Johnston Ridge,
  Coldwater Lake and Coldwater Peak.
• Discover fireweed and pearly everlasting meadows.
• Pockets of standing dead trees and blown-down forest give testimony
  to the power of the May 18, 1980 lateral blast.
• High country views of Mt. Whittier and Minnie Peak grace this trail.

Trail Facts: The trail heads west from Boundary Trail #1 through a
saddle to where it traverses to overlook standing-dead and blown-down
trees and views of construction activities. It then descends to
Coldwater Creek where it crosses via a bridge and connects to Lakes
trail #211.

Restricted Area: The trail is the restricted area boundary from the
junction with the Boundary Trail to 1/2 mile beyond the junction with
Lakes Trail #211. Travel allowed on approved trails only. Off-trail
travel and camping are prohibited to protect sensitive natural features
and scientific studies. Research permits are required for off-trail travel.

Considerations: Treat all drinking water along the trail.

Connections: Coldwater Trail #230 connects to Boundary Trail #1
and Lakes Trail #211 and provides cross-monument hiking opportunities.

Map: Spirit Lake West quadrangle.

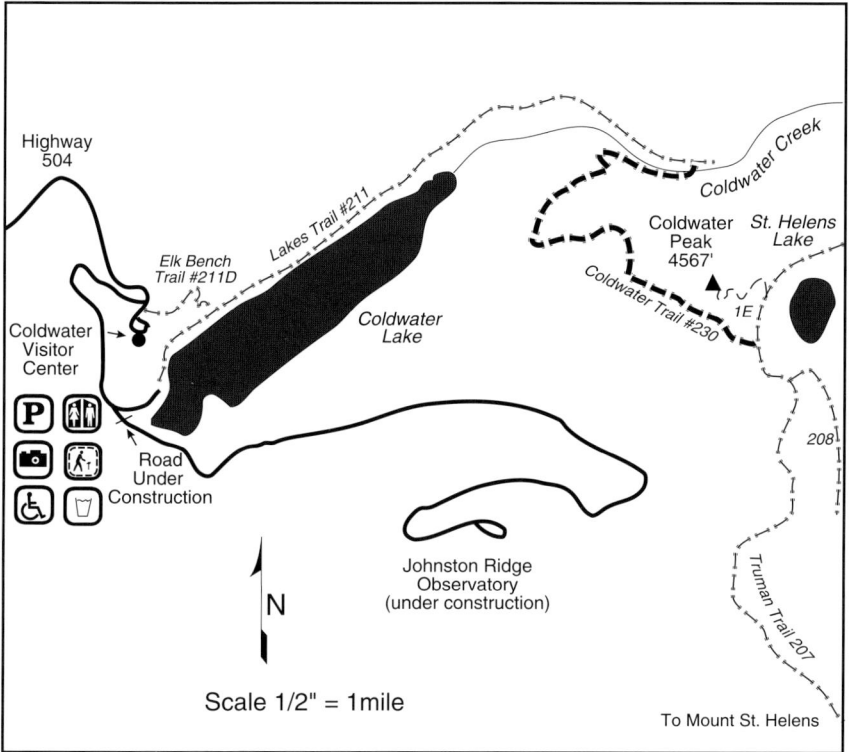

Trail of Two Forests #233

——— Users ——— Difficulty ——— Facilities ———

Location: Forest Road 8303
Length: 1/4 mile loop
Elevation: 1810 feet
Season: spring to late fall
Use: medium

Trail Talk:
- Discover the memory of a forest captured in basaltic lava when a fiery lava flow from Mount St. Helens engulfed and consumed the forest 1900 years ago.
- Stay on the boardwalk trail built to protect the fragile mosses and plants that struggle for life on the lava.
- Learn from the interpretive signs that tell the tale of two forests.
- Explore the cool dark interior of a horizontal tree cast. Flashlights recommended.
- Bring a picnic to enjoy beneath the shade of a lodgepole pine forest.

Trail Facts: This boardwalk trail is located through a 1900-year-old lava flow. The scenic loop takes you to many examples of vertical molds and also provides an opportunity to explore a horizontal mold left by a tree.

Considerations: The area's plant life is very fragile, so please stay on the boardwalk.

Connections:
- There are no direct connections. Ape Cave, another interesting geological feature to explore, is located nearby on Forest Road 8303.

Map: Mt. Mitchell quadrangle.

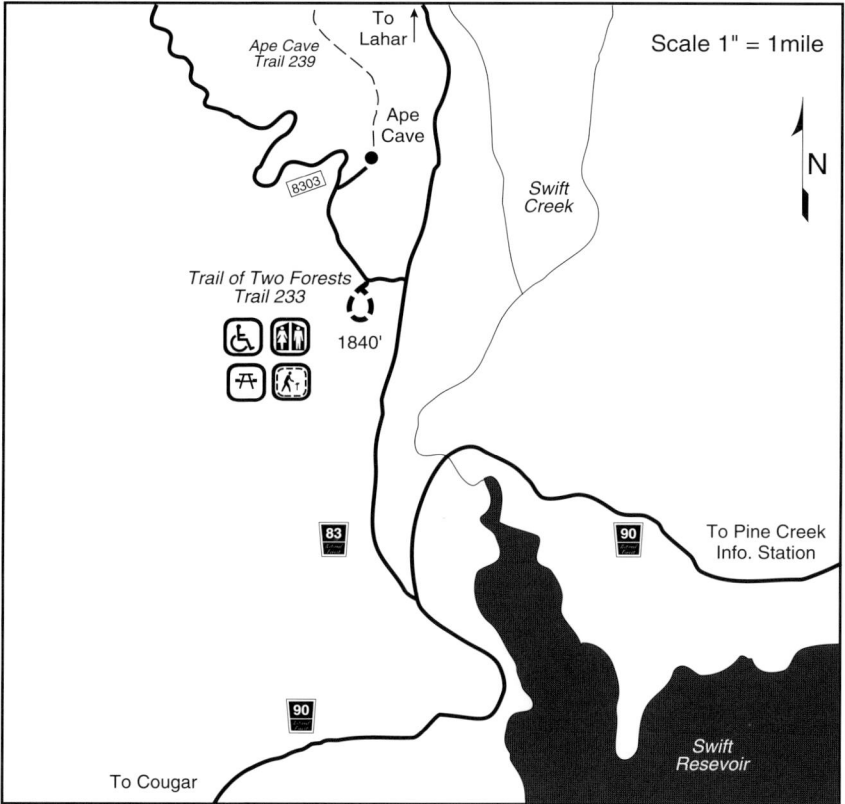

Ape Canyon Trail #234

──────── Users ──────── Difficulty ──────── Facilities ────────

Location: begins, Ape Canyon Trailhead, Forest Rd. 83; ends, Loowit Trail #216
Length: 5.5 miles (one way)
Elevation: 3100 feet, low point; 4200 feet, high point
Season: summer to fall
Use: medium

Trail Talk:
• Walk along the edge of a large mudflow from the 1980 eruption. Compare the terrain swept by the mudflow with the untouched area traversed by the trail.
• Hike through a growing plantation of young trees; then enter one of the few remaining segments of old growth forest untouched by the blast or mudflows.
• Catch magnificent views of Mt. Adams from grassy meadows on the east side of the ridge. Observe the wildflowers and watch for mountain goats which have been sighted in this area.

Trail Facts: This maintained trail begins at the crumbling edge of a mudflow and then follows an old road through a young regenerating forest. It then climbs through a remnant of old growth forest and emerges into open meadows on the east side of the ridge. It continues along the ridge through patches of old growth and standing dead trees and climbs to open meadows and volcano scoured rock at the top of Ape Canyon, where it terminates at the junction with Loowit Trail #216.

Considerations:
• This trail has a steady upward grade as it climbs to Ape Canyon. Beware of steep drops and loose rock in the Ape Canyon area at the top of the trail.

Connections: The Ape Canyon Trail connects with the Loowit Trail #216 for access to the Windy Ridge area or a round-the-mountain hike. This trail is part of a popular loop for mountain bikers: starting at Windy Ridge, ride the Truman Trail #207 to Abraham Trail #216D, then continue south to the Loowit Trail #216 and follow the Loowit Trail to the junction at the top of Ape Canyon Trail.

Map: Smith Creek Butte and Mount St. Helens quadrangles.

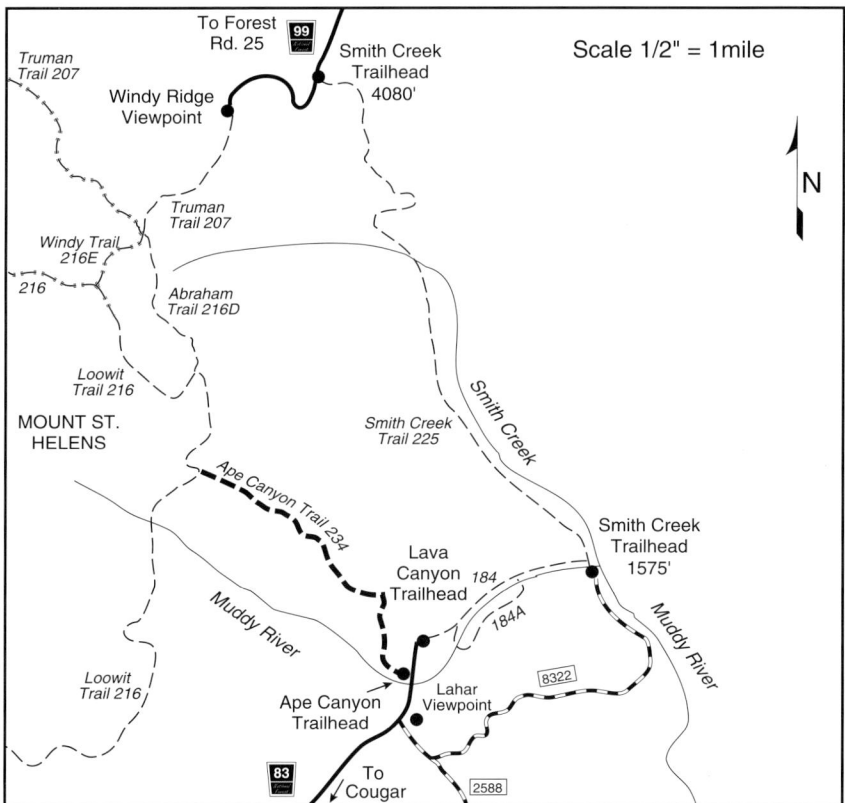

Blue Lake Horse Trail #237

Location: begins and ends along the Toutle Trail #238
Length: 5.25 miles (one way)
Elevation: 2600 feet, low point
Season: May–November
Use: medium

Trail Talk:
• Enjoy spectacular views of Mount St. Helens.
• Ride through lodgepole pine forest that gives way to Noble fir.
• Traverse the edge of a mudflow that swept down the west flanks of
  the mountain on May 18, 1980.

Trail Facts: The trail leaves Toutle Trail #238 at the 8100-600 Road
and crosses Road 8100 and gently climbs to another junction with
Toutle Trail #238. It continues to climb and then crosses the May 18,
1980 mudflow. The trail follows the west side of the mudflows and
then turns west through a managed forest to where the trail junctions
with Toutle Trail #238 one half mile south of Sheep Canyon Trail
#240.

Considerations: Water should be treated along the trail.

Connections: A short and a long loop opportunity exists with Toutle
Trail #238.

Map: Goat Mt. quadrangle

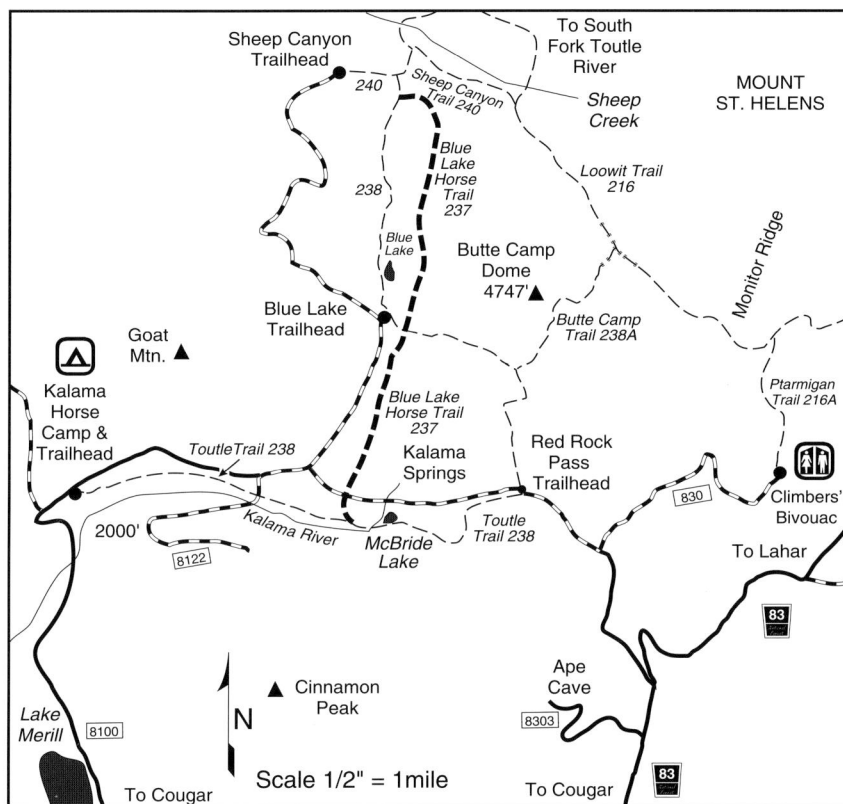

Sheep Canyon Trailhead

To South Fork Toutle River

MOUNT ST. HELENS

240

Sheep Canyon Trail 240

Sheep Creek

238

Blue Lake Horse Trail 237

Loowit Trail 216

Blue Lake

Butte Camp Dome 4747' ▲

Blue Lake Trailhead

Goat Mtn. ▲

Butte Camp Trail 238A

Monitor Ridge

Kalama Horse Camp & Trailhead

Ptarmigan Trail 216A

Blue Lake Horse Trail 237

ToutleTrail 238

Kalama Springs

Red Rock Pass Trailhead

Climbers' Bivouac

Kalama River

Toutle Trail 238

830

2000'

McBride Lake

To Lahar

8122

83

▲ Cinnamon Peak

Ape Cave

Lake Merill

8100

N

8303

Scale 1/2" = 1mile

To Cougar

83

To Cougar

Toutle Trail #238
Kalama River segment

──────── Users ──────── Difficulty ──────── Facilities ────────

Location: begins, Kalama Horse Camp, Forest Road 8100; ends, Red Rock Pass Trailhead, Forest Road 8100
Length: 5.6 miles (one way)
Elevation: 2070 feet, low point; 3120 feet, high point
Use: low

Trail Talk:
• Follow along the clear, spring-fed Kalama River as it passes through moss-carpeted lava flows and forests of Douglas-fir, western white, and lodgepole pine.
• Climb above McBride Lake and enjoy the view of Mount St. Helens.
• Explore a towering stand of majestic noble fir.

Trail facts: This maintained trail follows the course of the Kalama River. It begins at river level and then climbs above it onto an old lava flow. The trail then returns to river level until reaching McBride Lake. It then leaves the river and climbs above the lake. The trail connects into the next segment of the Toutle Trail at Red Rock Pass.

Considerations: All water should be treated for safe drinking.

Connections:
• Toutle Trail #238 continues on to the South Fork of the Toutle River.
• Toutle Trail #238 junctions with Blue Lake Horse Trail #237 creating several long and short loop opportunities for day and extended trips for pack and saddle users.

Map: Goat Mountain and Mount St. Helens quadrangles.

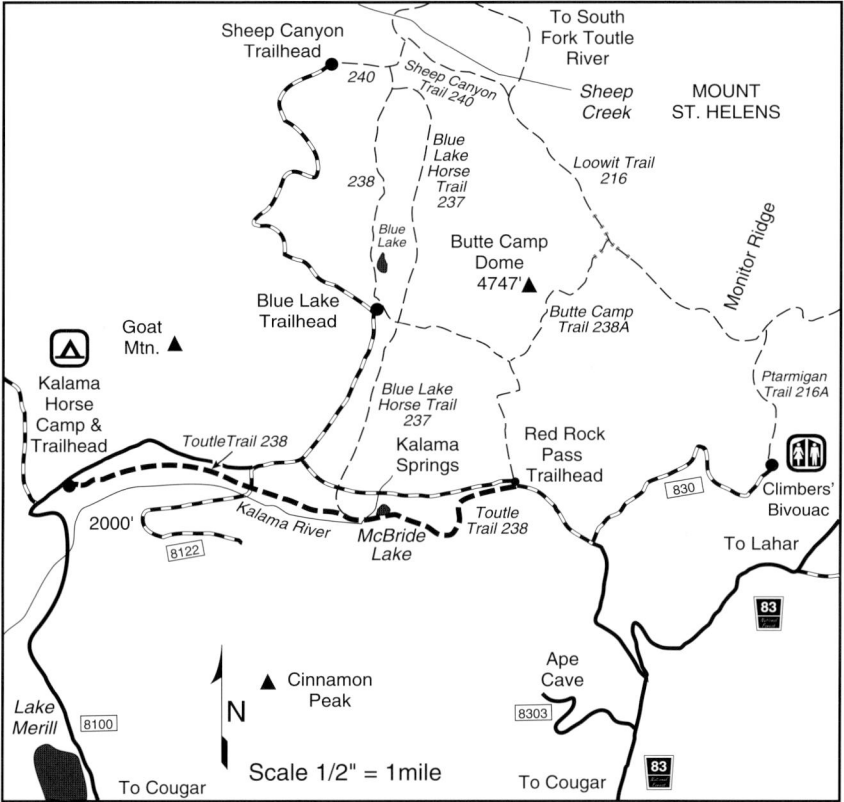

Sheep Canyon
Trailhead

To South
Fork Toutle
River

*Sheep
Creek*

MOUNT
ST. HELENS

240

*Sheep Canyon
Trail 240*

238

*Blue
Lake
Horse
Trail
237*

*Loowit Trail
216*

*Blue
Lake*

Butte Camp
Dome
4747' ▲

Monitor Ridge

Blue Lake
Trailhead

*Butte Camp
Trail 238A*

Goat
Mtn. ▲

Kalama
Horse
Camp &
Trailhead

*Blue Lake
Horse Trail
237*

Kalama
Springs

Red Rock
Pass
Trailhead

*Ptarmigan
Trail 216A*

830

Climbers'
Bivouac

ToutleTrail 238

2000'

Kalama River

8122

*McBride
Lake*

*Toutle
Trail 238*

To Lahar

83

N

▲ Cinnamon
Peak

Ape
Cave

8303

83

*Lake
Merill*

8100

Scale 1/2" = 1mile

To Cougar

To Cougar

Toutle Trail #238

———— Users ———— Difficulty ———— Facilities ————

Location: begins, Red Rock Pass Trailhead on Forest Road 8100 or
Blue Lake Trailhead Forest Road 8123-170 spur; ends, Loowit
Trail #216

Length: 3.0 miles from Red Rock Pass to Blue Lake Trailhead.
5.0 miles from Blue Lake Trailhead to Loowit Trail #216 (one way)

Elevation: 3116 feet, low point; 3540 feet, high point

Season: early summer to fall

Use: medium

Trail Talk:
• For those wanting excellent views of Mount St. Helens and to hike
the entire route, start at Red Rock Pass (Forest Road 81).
• Watch Mount St. Helens' history unfold as you travel over a massive
lava flow (1900 years old) and then wind in and out of lodgepole pine
forests while crossing recent and ancient mudflows.
• From the Blue Lake Trailhead on Forest Road 8123 a short (1/4-
mile) hike along Coldsprings Creek brings you to sapphire Blue Lake.
• At the Sheep Canyon Bridge, scan the canyon floor and see the
results of a mudflow that slammed from bank to bank as it carved its
way down this valley on May 18, 1980.
• The trail ends with a sweeping view of the volcano-impacted South
Fork Toutle River.

Trail Facts: This maintained trail ascends gradually as it follows along
Coldsprings Creek to Blue Lake. It then becomes relatively level as it
passes through an old-growth noble fir forest until climbing a ridge and
entering a regenerating clearcut. Beyond there, it descends through the
forest to Sheep Canyon. It terminates at the junction with Loowit Trail
#216, where you can view the South Fork of the Toutle River.

Considerations: This trail is popular with horse users. Horses are
not allowed beyond Sheep Canyon Bridge or on Butte Camp Trail
#238A. Water is available but should be treated for safe drinking.

Connections:

- This trail junctions with Butte Camp Trail #238A, Blue Lake Horse Trail #237, Sheep Canyon Trail #210 and Loowit Trail #216.
- Butte Camp is accessible by taking Trail #238A at its junction, 1/2 mile up Trail #238.
- Near Sheep Creek, Sheep Canyon Trail #240 continues up the canyon to the east and provides a loop opportunity by using Loowit Trail #216 and then reconnecting at the terminus of the Toutle Trail. Westward, Sheep Canyon Trail exits to Forest Road 8123.

Map: Goat Mountain and Mount St. Helens quadrangles.

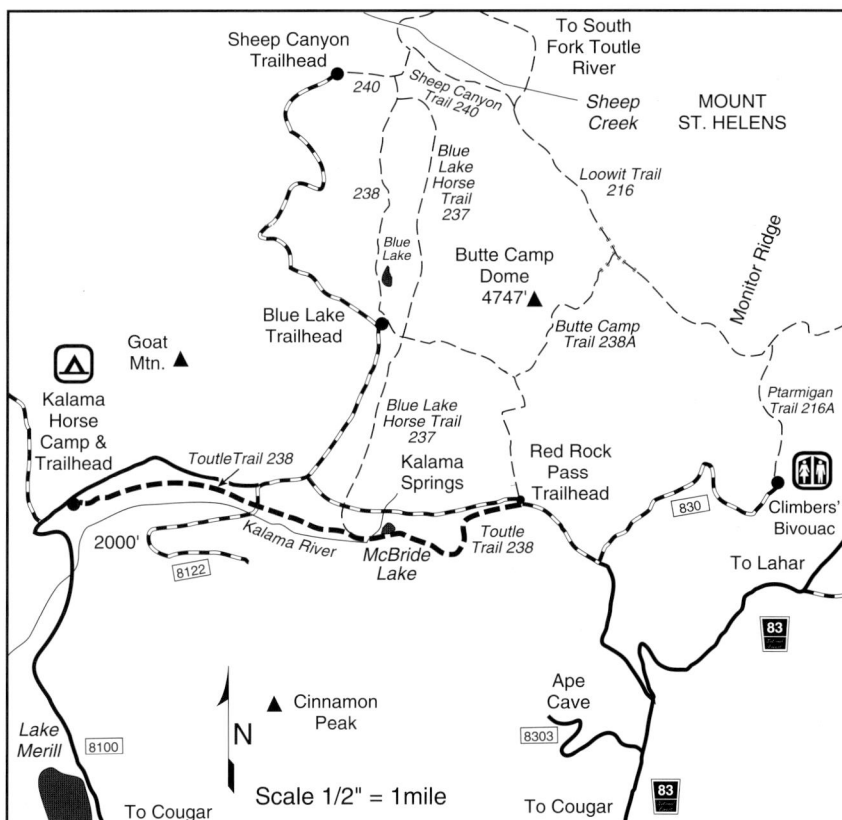

Butte Camp Trail #238A

——— Users ———   Difficulty   ——— Facilities ———

Location: begins, Toutle Trail #238; ends, Loowit Trail #216
Length: 2.7 miles (one way)
Elevation: 3520 feet, low point; 4800 feet, high point
Season: summer to fall
Use: medium

Trail Talk:
• Hike through geological time as you travel across a 1900-year-old lava flow, mudflows from the 1980 eruption and, if you desire, to the crater rim of a living volcano (permit required above the 4800 foot elevation).
• A short (1/8-mile) climb up the trail will reward you with an outstanding view of Mount St. Helens.
• Because of the relative ease, remarkable views, and the delicious berries that abound in summer, hikers of all ages can enjoy the first portion of this trail.
• Beyond 1 mile, the trail begins to climb gradually through a gnarled, lodgepole pine forest which has adapted to life on a crusty lava flow.
• Rest at Lower Butte Camp where an inviting meadow dotted with wildflowers lies nestled between two hillsides of noble fir.
• Climb to upper Butte Camp where you'll discover subalpine meadows, splendid views to the south, and the imposing flanks of Mount St. Helens dominating the skyline.

Trail Facts: This maintained trail traverses a lava flow and then enters a regenerating clearcut. It starts a steady climb through a lodgepole pine forest until reaching Lower Butte Camp. The trail then switchbacks up a hillside through a noble fir forest to the subalpine meadows of Upper Butte Camp.

Considerations: Upper Butte Camp is a sensitive research area. Please protect this site by camping only at Lower Butte Camp. Above

4800 feet in elevation a climbing permit is required. Those planning to climb Mount St. Helens can obtain more information from Mount St. Helens National Volcanic Monument Headquarters.

Restricted Area: Travel is allowed on approved trails only. Off-trail travel and camping are prohibited to protect sensitive natural features and scientific studies. Research permits are required for off-trail travel.

Connections:
• At the beginning of the Butte Camp Trail, Toutle Trail #238 veers off to the left.
• At the end, Butte Camp Trail junctions with Loowit Trail #216.

Map: Mount St. Helens quadrangle.

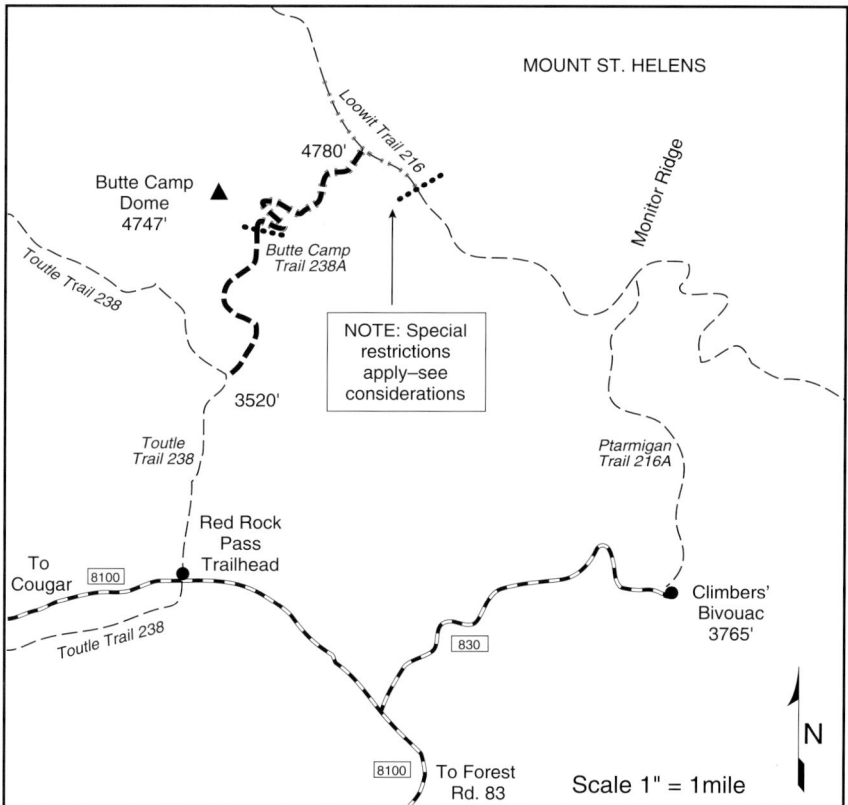

Ape Cave and Ape Cave Trail #239

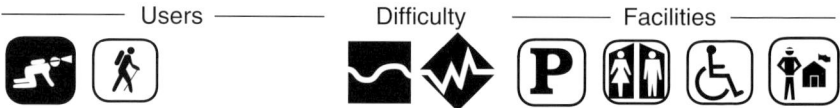

---------- Users ---------- Difficulty ---------- Facilities ----------

Location: Apes Headquarters, Forest Road 8303
Length: lower cave: 3/4 mile (one way); upper cave: 1 1/5 miles (one way); Ape Cave Trail: 1 mile (one way)
Elevation: 2115 feet
Season: year-round
Use: lower cave: high; upper cave: low

Trail Talk:

• Explore the longest intact lava tube in the continental United States.
• Ape Cave was discovered in 1951 by Lawrence Johnson and first explored by Harry Reese and his sons. The Reeses were members of an outdoor club called Mount St. Helens Apes. Hence the name, Ape Cave, a bit disappointing for those envisioning Bigfoot's den.
• Learn from the interpretive signs about the formation, unique features and the fragile life within a lava tube.
• There are two different routes of exploration inside the cave, plus an above-ground trail connecting the main and upper entrances.
• The lower cave is the easier and more popular route with its fairly level, mudflow-covered floor and unique features such as the "lava ball" wedged in the ceiling.
• The upper cave is for the more adventurous. This challenging hike climbs over large rock piles, scales an 8-foot lava fall and requires good balance and sturdy shoes.

Trail Facts: Lower cave is 3/4 miles long. Allow 1 1/4 hours to complete a round trip. Upper cave is 1 1/4 mile long, but you need to allow 2 1/2 hours for its exploration. The above-ground Ape Cave Trail (1 mile) will take you back to the main entrance. It's an easy level hike through the forest and also crosses some recent mudflows.

Considerations: Come prepared. Bring two sources of light, sturdy shoes, and warm clothing (even during summer, temperatures are 42

degrees.) Lantern rentals and guided interpretive walks are available
during the summer.

Connections:

• No direct connection, although the nearby Trail of Two Forests (1
  mile south) reveals more of the area's unique geology.

Map: Mt. Mitchell quadrangle.

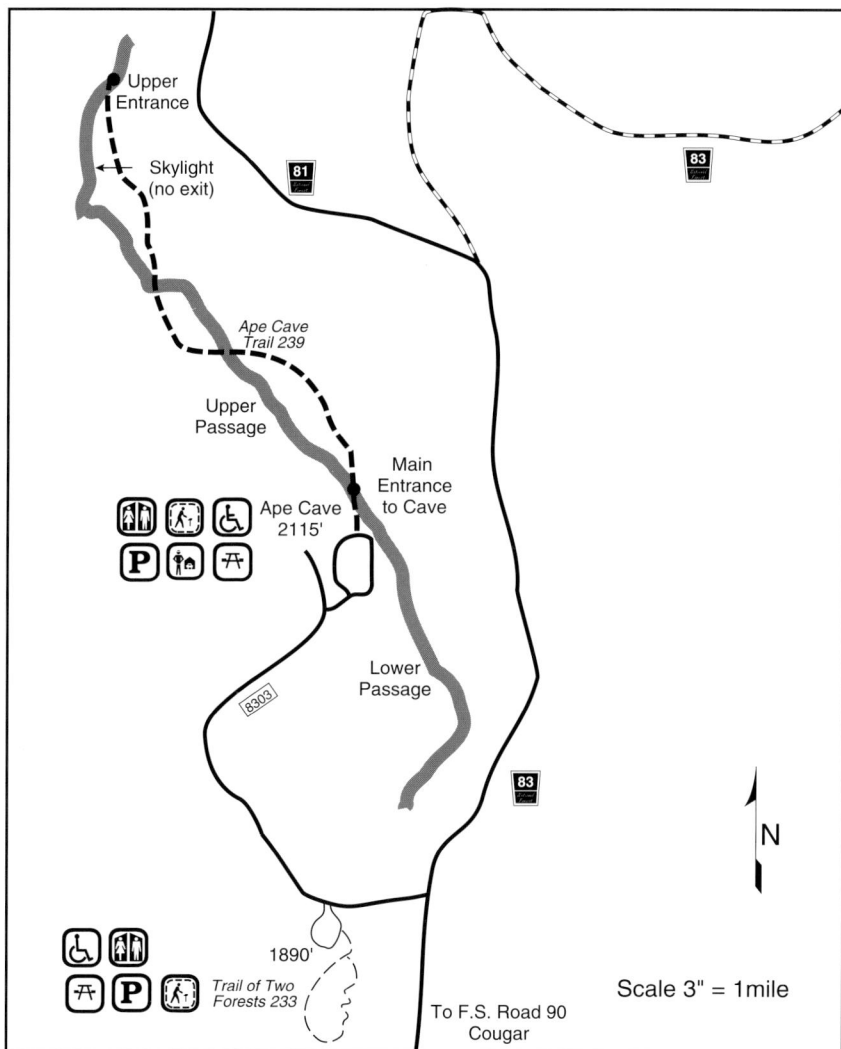

Sheep Canyon Trail #240

———— Users ———— Difficulty ———— Facilities ————

Location: begins, Sheep Canyon Trailhead on Forest Road 8123;
ends, Loowit Trail #216
Length: 2.2 miles (one way)
Elevation: 3400 feet, low point; 4600 feet, high point
Season: summer to fall
Use: low

Trail Talk:
• Take a side trip (1/4 mile) to view the volcano-ravaged Toutle River Valley.
• Hike up the trail through young trees and then enter the cool, dark interior of a towering noble fir forest.
• Discover a 75-foot ribbon of water streaming down a solid rock cliff.
• Notice evidence left by the 1980 eruption. An abrasive mudflow scoured the canyon to bedrock and bounced from bank to bank as it roared down the valley.
• Stop and appreciate the view from the bridge; a composition of Mount St. Helens framed by the steely gray canyon walls and the rich greens of a conifer forest.
• Witness the arrival of the first pioneer plants to take root in this new landscape.
• Enjoy one of the most dynamic hikes through a landscape changed by recent volcanic activity by following the loop opportunity described in "Connections."

Trail Facts: This maintained trail passes through an old clearcut and heads into a noble fir forest. It then follows along the canyon edge of Sheep Creek and junctions with the Toutle Trail before crossing the drainage (by bridge). After leaving the edge of the mudflow-scoured canyon, it passes through forest, over old lava flows, and terminates at the junction of Loowit Trail #216.

Considerations: Beware of steep dropoffs near the waterfalls.

Connections:

• For an excellent hike through a constantly changing volcanic landscape, follow Sheep Canyon Trail #240 to Loowit Trail #216 and turn north. The Loowit Trail junctions with Toutle Trail #238 near the South Fork Toutle River Valley. By following Toutle Trail #238 south you'll reconnect with Sheep Canyon Trail #240.

Map: Mount St. Helens and Goat Mountain quadrangles.

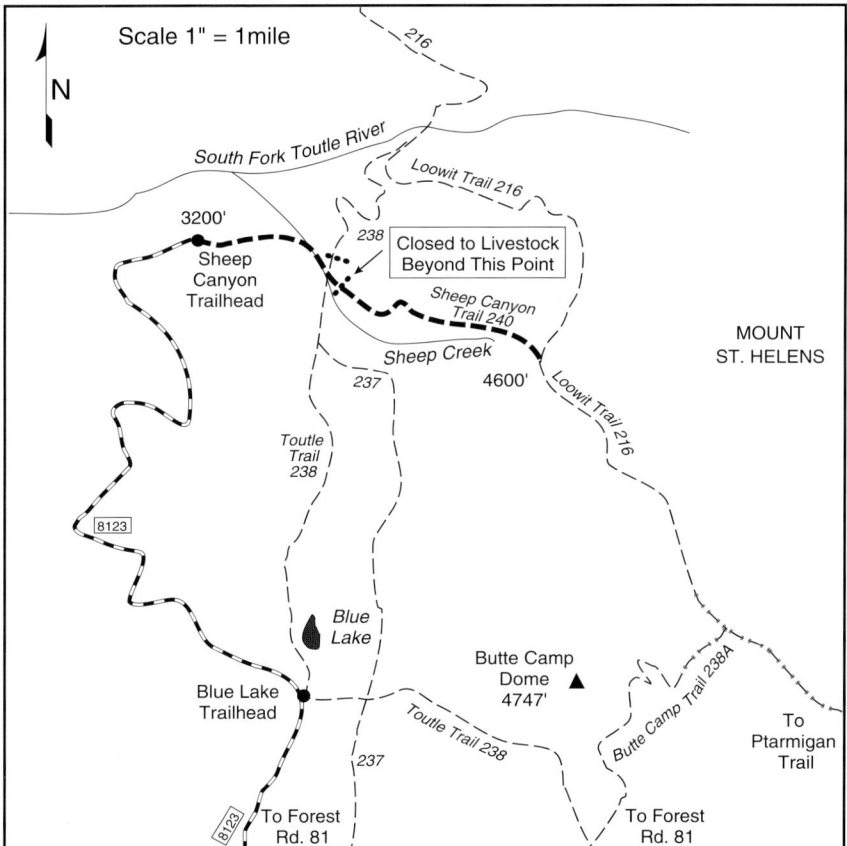

Windy Ridge Sand Ladder #242

———— Users ———— Difficulty ———— Facilities ————

Location: begins, Windy Ridge Viewpoint
Length: 0.25 miles (one way)
Elevation: 4170 feet, low point; 4270 feet, high point
Season: summer to fall
Use: high

Trail Talk:
• Ascend 365 steps to obtain a view into the crater of Mount St. Helens.

Considerations: Take care with your footing; the pumice can easily slip out from under your feet. This can be a strenuous climb because of the high elevation.

Connections:
• No direct connections.

Map: Spirit Lake West, Spirit Lake East, Mount St. Helens, and Smith Creek Butte quadrangles.

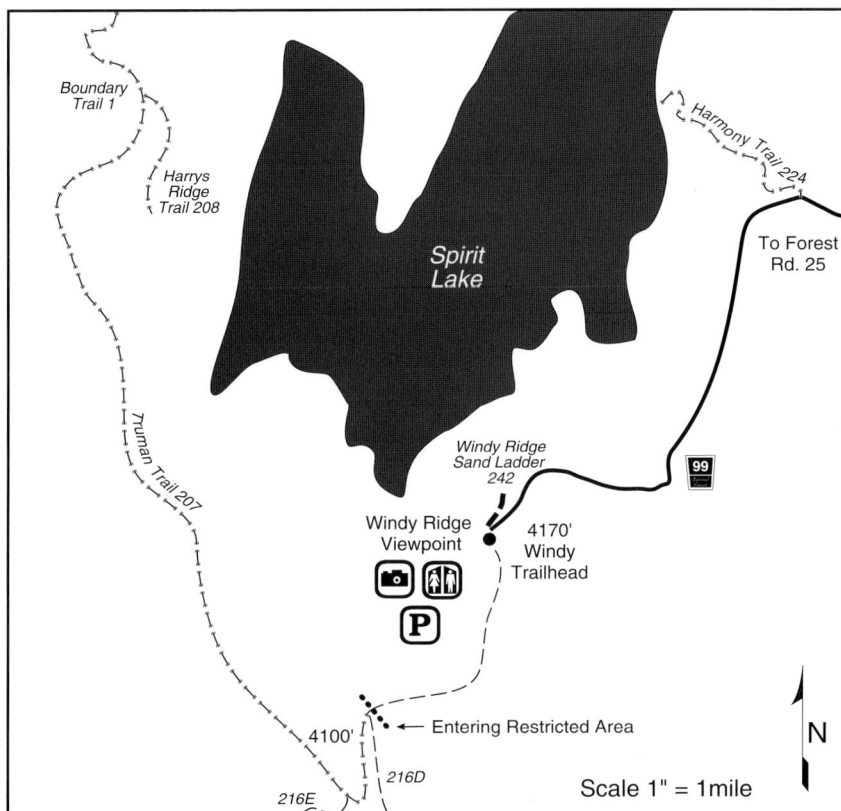

Boundary
Trail 1

Harmony Trail 224

Harrys
Ridge
Trail 208

Spirit
Lake

To Forest
Rd. 25

Truman Trail 207

Windy Ridge
Sand Ladder
242

99

Windy Ridge
Viewpoint

4170'
Windy
Trailhead

P

4100'

← Entering Restricted Area

N

216D

216E

Scale 1" = 1mile

Emergency Assistance

For emergency assistance, use the telephones at the following locations: climbers' bivouac, Marble Mountain Sno-Park, and Pine Creek Information Center. These telephones automatically dial the Emergency Dispatch Center. Commercial telephones may be found in Cougar.

Weather Information

It is suggested you call for current weather information before your hike. For the local weather forecast, call Weatherline at (503) 236-7575. NOAA weather radio also provides continuous weather forecasts and warnings. Those with special high-band FM radios can tune to frequencies 162.550 and 162.475 for information. If you will be hiking in steep areas with snow, current snow avalanche information can be received by calling (503) 326-2400.

Be informed:

• Contact Mount St. Helens National Volcanic Monument for the most recent update on existing conditions.

Mount St. Helens Visitor Center
3029 Spirit Lake Memorial Highway
Castle Rock, WA 98611
(206) 274-2100

Mount St. Helens NVM
42218 NE Yale Bridge Road
Amboy, WA 98601
(206) 750-3900

U.S. Geological Survey
5400 MacArthur
Vancouver, WA 98661
(206) 696-7694